COMMERCIAL
REAL ESTATE INVEST

COMMERCIAL REAL ESTATE INVESTING

A Creative Guide to Successfully Making Money

DOLF DE ROOS

WILEY

John Wiley & Sons, Inc.

Published by John Wiley & Sons, Inc., Hoboken, New Jersey.
Published simultaneously in Canada.

For general information on our other products and services or for technical support, please contact our Customer Care Department within the United States at (800) 762-2974, outside the United States at (317) 572-3993 or fax (317) 572-4002.

Wiley also publishes its books in a variety of electronic formats. Some content that appears in print may not be available in electronic books. For more information about Wiley products, visit our web site at www.wiley.com.

Library of Congress Cataloging-in-Publication Data:
de Roos, Dolf.
   Commercial real estate investing : a creative guide to successfully making money / Dolf de Roos.
      p.   cm.
   ISBN 978-0-470-22738-1 (pbk.)
   1. Commercial real estate.   2. Real estate investment.   I. Title.
   HD1393.55.D47 2008
   332.63′24—dc22

                                                         2007039477

Printed in the United States of America.

10 9 8 7 6 5 4 3 2 1

Contents

Preface

Anyone with $20 million in his pocket can go out and buy a $20 million real estate portfolio. This book is not for those people—it is for those with little or even nothing in their pockets, who want to go out and make a fortune anyway.

Of course, if $20 million is just a little to you, you can still benefit from this book and learn how to easily acquire $200 million or more of real estate. In my experience, though, people with this kind of cash often do not have the time or inclination to do so. Therefore, those with no money and lots of drive may do well teaming up with people with lots of money and no inclination, to form a truly symbiotic investment partnership.

Beware, however, that your perception as to what constitutes a lot of money inevitably changes as you start to accumulate some. While this book focuses on how you can amass a fortune, remember that in a hundred years' time, how much you will have made will not be of much importance to anyone. In the final analysis, how much fun you have along the way could be the ultimate reward. That is why I say, above all else, be curious, learn something new each day, help other people, be grateful, and have fun!

Successful investing!

Dolf de Roos

August 2007

Acknowledgments

My passion for commercial real estate has been inspired and fueled by many people. While my thoughts, theories, and methods have been formulated over many years, countless people have—wittingly or unwittingly—contributed to my thinking, from real estate agents, bankers, mortgage brokers, and appraisers, to tenants, members of real estate investment associations, accountants, and literally thousands of investors (both budding and experienced) who have honored me by attending my events and who have forced me to expand my thinking.

While it is impossible to acknowledge everyone, many people deserve and have my deep appreciation. If I have missed you, then I apologize in advance; know that my appreciation is real nonetheless.

Sincere thanks go to Jay Abraham, Anthony Aoun, John Baen, Wayne Bourke, James Burgin, Randy Carder, Stephen Collins, Allen and Kenina Court, Keith and Sandi Cunningham, Curt Denny, Ross Denny, Craig Donnell, Charles Drace, Cary Ferguson,

Andy Fuehl, Paul Gibbard, Andrew Gibbons, Daniel Godden, Pepi Gomez, Anthony Gough, David Grose, Datuk Maznah Hamid, Laurie Harting, Paige Hemmis, Dave Henderson, Adrian Heyman, Ian Jackson, Larry Jellen, Bob Jones, Stefan Kasian, Cindy Kenney, Rich Lamphere, Patrick Liew, Dave and Vicki Lovegrove, Katie Moustakas, Nick McCaw, Wayne and Lynn Morgan, Mike Pero, Craig Peters, Neale Petersen, Kean Pitcairn, Jim Poignand, Carrie Putman, Trevor Quirk, Tony Robbins, Alex Rodriguez, Paul Roussell, Trevi Sawalich, Constantine Scurtis, Mike Sexton, Bill Shopoff, Scott Sullivan, Garrett Sutton, David and Julia Sykes, Richard and Veronica Tan, Brian Tracy, Donald Trump, Dr. Robert Tybon, Andrew Waite, Jon Ward, Tung Desem Waringin, Richard Watters, Ron Whiteley, and Paul Wright.

Notes on Reading This Book

Numerous photos are included in this book to illustrate properties being discussed or points being made. Because of printing constraints, these photos are reproduced in black and white. Full-color versions of these photos, as well as other supporting documentation, photos, and newspaper articles, can be found on the web site www.dolfderoos.com.

Many examples of real estate bought or negotiated are discussed, ranging in value from $59,000 to hundreds of millions of dollars. As this book is intended for those who are relatively new to commercial real estate, an emphasis has been placed on using modest examples of properties that hopefully are within the comfort zone of most readers. Bear in mind, however, that the effort required to complete an $80,000 deal is about the same as that required to complete an $80 million deal, so do not intend to focus on smaller properties forever.

Finally, please accept that any instances of words like *he, she, his,* or *her,* unless specifically referring to a person of known gender, are generic. Sometimes it is too cumbersome to write "he or she" or "his or her portfolio," but the points being made apply to anyone.

Introduction

If you think commercial real estate is just like residential real estate except that you need more capital to get started, you are in for a surprise. Commercial real estate is completely different and often requires little or no capital.

If you think, like the masses, that commercial real estate is risky because you have often seen vacant commercial premises and thanked your lucky stars that you are not the owner, you are in for a shock. For reasons that I am excited to share in this book, I *seek out* vacant commercial buildings, as I have figured out a way of making money, huge sums of it, seemingly out of thin air, by doing something very straightforward with these vacant buildings—*something that you cannot do with residential buildings*.

If you think commercial real estate is too complex, too specialized, too esoteric, and too difficult for you to even consider, then let me take you on a journey to convince you that it is none of these things. In fact, I firmly believe that after reading this book, you will no longer want to even consider residential real estate as an investment option, and will focus instead on commercial real estate with both enthusiasm and confidence. The only regret you may have is that you didn't discover this information sooner.

Consider this: Of all the wealthy ($100 million-plus net worth) property investors I have come across in over 30 years of investing and teaching real estate in more than 25 countries (I have had the privilege of working with many prominent people in real estate all over the world), at most two have made their fortune through residential property—the rest have all done it through commercial property.

Think about this. You wouldn't choose a surgeon with a low patient survival rate when there are others with a high survival rate. You wouldn't choose a car with a low crash-test rating over one with a high rating, or a school for your kids with a low graduation rate over one with a high graduation rate. So now that you know that nearly all wealthy property investors have achieved their wealth through commercial real estate, how can you justify even thinking of buying one more residential property? It would be like dropping your kids off at a bad school, and driving yourself in an unsafe car to a hospital to have surgery performed on you by a surgeon with a low patient survival rate. That is nuts, right? Well, in relative terms, so is investing in residential real estate.

This last fact alone should be enough to convince you to convert to commercial real estate, and you could save yourself a lot of time by not having to read the rest of this book if you converted on that basis. However, you would miss out on a lot of fun, which brings me to my next point.

If you think commercial real estate is dry and boring, and the only reason you'd even consider it is that it is lucrative, then you are in for a real surprise. Residential real estate, for reasons I explain in this book, can be repetitious and therefore somewhat bland, but commercial real estate has so many opportunities for creativity, thinking outside of the box, and coming up with wacky ideas, that it genuinely is a lot of fun. At any rate, after I present my case, you can decide for yourself.

In case you think that I am contradicting myself and the 10 books I have written on residential real estate, think again. I stand by everything I have said in those books: Residential real estate truly is, in my opinion, a much better investment than stocks, bonds, mutual funds, Treasury bills, certificates of deposit, commodities, options, futures, and unit trusts, for reasons that I have explained in some detail in those books. However, when faced with a choice between residential and commercial real estate, I would recommend commercial real estate as your way to riches. Certainly, with my own investing, I have long ago focused almost exclusively on commercial properties, for reasons that I share in this book.

There are, of course, many ways of investing in commercial real estate, as evidenced by the number of existing books on the subject. You will find this book to be different. The fact that I have a different approach, philosophy, and strategy does not, however, invalidate others. You may successfully implement the ideas in this book, and you could also successfully implement the ideas of other commercial real estate books. (You may also be unsuccessful in either case, although it is difficult to fail in real estate as the market is so forgiving of tactical errors.)

At the end of the day, it is not just knowing a strategy, but how you implement it, that can be the difference between a successful experience and a learning experience. If you have an angry, gruff, stern, and rude nature, you could go on vacation to some exotic place and conclude that all the locals are angry, gruff, stern, and rude. Similarly, if you are optimistic, happy, bright, and charming, you will more than likely conclude that the locals are just that. The reason, in both cases, should be obvious: How you act, behave, and treat others will largely determine how others act, behave, and treat you. In this way, we create our own reality.

If you believe that commercial real estate is difficult, requires huge amounts of capital, will involve you in endless trauma, and will burden you with stifling vacancies, then those beliefs will manifest themselves in your life. If, however, perhaps with the aid of this book, you believe that commercial real estate is inherently interesting, remarkably simple, an opportunity to help many people, a vehicle for releasing your latent and pent-up creativity, unbelievably lucrative, and a lot of fun on top of it all, then those beliefs will manifest themselves in your life.

Let me show you why I like commercial real estate.

CHAPTER 1

Just What Is Commercial Real Estate?

From the outset, we need to agree on exactly what constitutes commercial real estate.

We may all agree that a four-bedroom, three-bathroom residence is residential real estate, and that a block of four shops is commercial real estate, but what about a block of 10 units in an apartment complex that both the bank and broker classify as commercial real estate? The fact is, for reasons that seem to me to be entirely arbitrary, where there are four or more units in a residential complex, the building is often classified as commercial for mortgage and insurance purposes and for transaction commissions. What about industrial properties, such as an assembly plant, paint shop, or warehouse; or hospitality properties such as hotels, motels, or amusement parks? Are they in yet other categories?

1

And what about specialist properties such as a quarry, a hospital, an airport, or a rocket launchpad?

Let me therefore make it perfectly clear what I mean by *residential* and *commercial* real estate. I know that simplifying things is not very popular these days, but for the purposes of this book, I want to make the following definitions:

Residential real estate is real estate where people live (in residences!).

Commercial real estate is real estate where commerce is conducted.

Based on this simple and sensible concept, it becomes easy to categorize any piece of real estate. Houses, individual apartments, apartment complexes, condominiums, duplexes, and triplexes are clearly all residential real estate. Conversely, shops, offices, assembly plants, paint shops, warehouses, hotels, motels, amusement parks, quarries, hospitals, airports, and rocket launchpads are all commercial real estate.

In case you want to argue that hotels, motels, and student accommodation should, by my definition, all be classified as residential real estate, as people quite clearly live there, then note the following subtle distinction. The operators of hotels, motels, and student accommodation are definitely renting out short-term residential accommodation to their clients. However, if you lease your building to a hotel, motel, or student accommodation operator on a long-term commercial lease, then from your point of view, your tenants conduct a commercial operation there, and these properties are all examples of commercial real estate.

What if three doctors operate their medical practice out of what was formerly a home? Well, they are not living there, and commerce is conducted, so it is commercial. What if a carpet factory is converted into loft accommodation? In this case, the use is for residential purposes, so it is residential. Be prepared for many more examples of blatant simplicity in this book.

Just as residential real estate can be further subdivided into categories such as freestanding single-family homes, single-story multiunits, and multistory apartment complexes, so can commercial real estate be further subdivided into categories such as industrial, hospitality, office space, retail, and specialist. The feature these categories all have in common, though, is that commerce is conducted there. The significance of that distinction will become apparent as we proceed.

CHAPTER 2

People versus Contracts

For some reason that I cannot understand, most of the people I have met or taught in the past two decades (and we are talking about literally hundreds of thousands of people) think that commercial real estate works just like residential real estate, except that the dollars involved are much larger, and that the potential risks and problems are also much larger. In order to convince you that both assumptions are wrong, we will explore real estate from a number of different angles throughout this book.

There are in fact many differences between residential and commercial real estate from legal, practical, and operational points of view, all of which, without exception, make commercial real estate a far superior investment. We discuss these differences in Chapter 3. For now, I want to highlight the biggest fundamental difference between residential and commercial real estate. Philosophically, with residential real estate, you are dealing with *people*, whereas with commercial real estate, you are dealing with *contracts*.

Before you counter by saying that you have seen a residential tenancy agreement (a contract!) and know of at least one commercial tenant who has met with his landlord (a person!), I want to stress that I am speaking *philosophically*. Of course there is paperwork involved with residential real estate—application forms, background check authority forms, tenancy agreements, and so forth. And of course commercial real estate involves dealing with people—brokers, property managers, leasing agents, and the like. However, in essence, when you own residential properties, as I suspect you already may, you end up spending a lot of time talking with people.

You get a call from a tenant telling you that a faucet is leaking, and you have to negotiate a time to have it repaired; 9 A.M. on Friday does not suit him, 4 P.M. on Thursday does not suit you, and bingo, you are dealing with people. You get a letter from the local council telling you that the grass is too long at one of your properties, and you have to call the tenant to get him to do something about it. The tenant, of course, swears that he just cut it the week before, so what is all the fuss about? You counter by saying that nonetheless you have this letter from the council requiring action—and, just like I said, you are dealing with people. You get a call about a blocked toilet. You tell the tenants this is the third time in two months, and what on earth are they putting in there to cause it to block, to which they reply that it's none of your business, just fix it—and hey, presto, you are dealing with people. Residential real estate by its very nature involves dealing with people.

Now in case you are thinking, "I am a people person, I like people, so what is the big deal?" let me tell you that most people who decide to get out of residential real estate do so because they simply get fed up dealing with all the people and their incessant complaints, tardiness, whining, avoidance, carelessness, rudeness, indifference, hang-ups, foibles, idiosyncrasies, and lack of respect for other people and their property.

Furthermore, in case you are thinking, "Has Dolf not heard about property managers?" let me respond by saying that I endorse and encourage the use of property managers, especially with residential real estate. However, while they serve as a buffer between you and your tenants, the fact remains that residential real estate is a people-centric business, and now you are dependent on the interpersonal skills of your property manager (who may not have your interest at heart the way you do) to deal with all your tenant issues such as scheduling a time to fix the leaking faucet, debating whether the grass needs to be cut, or discussing what is causing the lavatory to block so often. If these issues do not get handled promptly and properly, the situation can quickly escalate out of control. The point is not whether it is you or the property manager who ends up dealing with people (the tenants). Rather, the point is that residential real estate is, by its nature and by governmental and local body regulation, essentially a people-centric operation.

Commercial real estate, by contrast, is in essence driven by contracts. The central contract is, of course, the lease document, which may run to well over 100 pages on large premises and goes into a lot of detail on every aspect of the tenancy. For instance, you will never be phoned about a leaking faucet, as most commercial lease documents have a clause stipulating that it is the tenant's responsibility to keep the premises in a fully functioning condition and, further, that at the end of the tenancy, the premises will be handed back in exactly the same condition it was in at the beginning of the tenancy, except for normal wear and tear. Thus, most commercial tenants know and are entirely comfortable with the idea that they have to fix leaking faucets, replace burned-out light bulbs and fluorescent tubes, repair broken locks, clean carpets, and repair any damages to the property.

In fact, with most commercial lease documents, the landlord is only responsible for maintaining the building in a watertight condition (no leaking roofs or walls). Thus, painting the exterior, refurbishing the interior, and maintaining the grounds are the responsibility of the tenant. In Chapter 3 we explore why commercial tenants not only agree to this, but *want to do it*.

With residential real estate, you may specify that rent has to be paid on the first of every month, and you may even get away with a $25 late payment penalty in some jurisdictions, but what if they still don't pay? Depending on where you live, your options could be severely limited. In California, for instance, you cannot take any significant action to evict them until 90 days after the rent has been in default—90 days, despite the fact that they signed a tenancy agreement to pay on the first of each month! If you fill your car's tank at a gas station and then drive off before paying, it is considered theft; the police will be dispatched to arrest you straight away, and no one would think that the arrest was unwarranted. And yet, after signing an agreement to pay rent on time, legislators have sanctioned a tenant not paying rent for 90 days before you can take any significant action.

With commercial real estate, the lease document covers most bases. For example, it may stipulate that the rent has to be paid on the first of each month, and it may have clauses adding that if the rent is late there will be a late payment fee, plus interest will accrue at the monthly rate of 1 percent of the amount outstanding. Furthermore, if the rent is still not paid within two weeks of the due date, then (depending on the jurisdiction) the landlord shall have the right to *distrain* for rent—meaning you can enter the premises; seize all machinery and inventory (but not staff, of course); change the locks; and force the tenant to pay up or risk losing his seized assets, which you can sell to recover what is owed to you.

Throughout this book we uncover more examples of how residential real estate is people-centric and how commercial real estate is contract-centric. For now, just know that when you deal with commercial property, all the people aspects that have plagued you throughout your residential real estate career will be left behind, and you can deal with the clarity and certainty of contracts.

CHAPTER 3

Why Invest in Commercial Real Estate?

To understand why your real estate investing energy should be focused on commercial real estate, let's compare specific aspects of commercial real estate and residential real estate. This comparison is a valuable exercise in that most readers are probably familiar with the residential situation but not with the commercial analogue. In fact, I predict that some of the realities of commercial real estate will be a surprise to you, and a pleasant one at that. Let us begin.

Lease Duration

A residential tenancy is often month-to-month, or it may last for six months, occasionally a year, and more rarely two years. Commercial leases, by contrast, are very rarely month-to-month—usually only at the end of a longer lease, when the two parties have not arranged to sign a new lease. Typically, a commercial lease will be for two years, or three, or five, or longer. In fact, in the city of London, lease lengths of 25 years (yes, we are talking about a quarter of a century) were common until very recently. Leases of 10, 15, or 20 years are common for large premises or companies such as banks and large retailers.

Given that lease durations are longer with commercial real estate, let's explore the consequences for your portfolio as well as the underlying reasons why commercial tenants want longer leases, to help you understand why commercial real estate is so attractive.

The consequences for your portfolio should be obvious. Longer lease durations mean fewer lease renewals, and fewer searches for new tenants. If you have a tenant with six years remaining on a 10-year lease, then you know that for the next six years (barring the tenant going into bankruptcy) you will have an uninterrupted stream of rental income. That gives a tremendous sense of certainty. It enables you to project your finances into the future, calculate your margins, and expand your portfolio with confidence.

The sweet irony is that this benefit to you of long lease durations does not come at the expense of the tenant. In fact, most savvy commercial tenants *want* long leases, and until you grasp this concept, you will not fully embrace commercial real estate.

In general, commercial tenants derive their income on your premises. If there is an element of public interaction with the premises (for instance, it is a retail outlet and clients have been shopping there for years), then there is an intangible benefit called *goodwill* that is inherently built up in the premises. If the tenants had to shift location, they would lose a lot of their clients. Therefore, one of their fears with a lease renewal is that you as landlord will tell them that you will no longer lease the premises to them. As a result, it is the commercial tenants who are inclined to ask for long lease terms.

I commonly have tenants contact my office (or any of our property managers in various parts of the world) in the middle of a lease term, asking for—and sometimes pleading for—a longer lease. For instance, they may be halfway through a 10-year lease, and they will ask for the lease to be modified so that they still have 10 or 15 years to go before the lease comes up for renewal. Why would they want this? There are generally two reasons.

One reason is that they may be considering spending a lot of money refurbishing the premises, but they will do so only if they can be sure that they will have more than the remaining few years on the lease to get the benefit of their renovations. So the offer from the tenant essentially is, "If you let me pay you rent for at least another ten years, then I will spend a quarter of a million dollars on your property." How can you refuse an offer like that? They are not saying, "We will spend some money on your property, but only if you cut the remaining lease length in half." They want a *long* lease!

The second reason they may request a longer lease is if they are contemplating selling the business. If it is a thriving business of many years' standing, then both the business seller (your present tenant) and the potential buyer will know that there is the aforementioned goodwill built up in the premises. If the business is to be sold with only 18 months remaining on the lease, the buyer will be reluctant to pay much for the business, just in case you as landlord do not renew the lease. With a new lease expiry date, the business will be easier to sell, and it can be sold at a much higher price. And should you be at all concerned about a new business owner being responsible for the lease? Not at all! As we will see shortly, the sale of your tenant's business gives you one more layer of certainty that you will be able to collect the rent.

About a month ago, a tenant who operates a 24-hour convenience store in a block of shops submitted a proposal to extend his lease from 5 years remaining to a massive 20 years remaining. Whether he wants to make alterations to the building or sell the business, I am not quite sure and, frankly, I don't really care either way. He got what he wanted (a longer lease), and in granting that, my portfolio was strengthened. This is, of course, a classic win-win situation.

Similarly, when I was negotiating the purchase of a funeral home, which I have now owned for the better part of two decades, I remember sitting down with a potential tenant and presenting my expectations as to rental per square foot on the commercial portion, on the house that came with the premises, and on the garages. He didn't challenge me at all on the figures, but did come back, as if by counteroffer, by saying, "Well, I will only do this if you give me a long-term lease." At the time I would have been happy with a five-year lease, but rather than propose that, I simply asked him, "How long would you like?" to which he replied, "I will only do this if you give me a ten-year lease with a right of renewal for another ten years." He signed up for the 20 years that day.

Hopefully you are starting to get the picture that with commercial real estate, it is generally in the interest of both the tenant and the landlord to have longer, rather than shorter, lease terms.

Assignment of Lease

While on the subject of leases, consider this. If a residential tenant is partway through his one-year lease but gets a job offer in another city, he is still obligated to pay the rent until the end of the lease. If, however, he finds a substitute tenant who is willing to take over the lease, most landlords will agree to such a switch. What happens, though, if the new tenant defaults on rent payments? Can you go back to the original tenant to extract the rent? Of course not! You agreed to the substitution, and you have to pursue the new tenant for the defaulting rent.

With commercial real estate leases, if a tenant sells his business, such a sale must first of all be approved by the landlord, and second, if the new tenant is in default of his rent, you *can* go back to the original tenant and collect the rent from him. When a tenant sells his business, apart from the sale contract between the seller and the buyer, there is an "Assignment of Lease" contract between the seller, the buyer, and the landlord. This Assignment of Lease references the original lease, notes any modifications agreed to (more often than not there will be none), gives the landlord's consent to the buyers taking over the position of the sellers, and still holds liable the sellers in case the buyers are in default of their obligations under the terms of the original lease.

Why do most commercial lease documents around the world allow for these rules? The answer is simply that a commercial lease is seen as a serious commitment. About the only way of getting out of paying the rent on a commercial lease is if the tenant (or business) goes bankrupt. Without these rules, if a commercial tenant wanted to get out of paying the rent, all he would have to do is sell the business to someone at random for a dollar and walk away. When the seller of a business knows that he is effectively underwriting the new business (at least as far as rent payments are concerned) until the lease expires, he has a vested interest in finding a buyer who can actually run the business profitably. So every time a business is sold during a lease term, you, as landlord, have another layer of assurance that the rent will be paid.

The business that in my 30 years of experience in this game has the highest turnover of operators is a humble fish-and-chips shop. Why the turnover should be so high I do not know—it is

Figure 3.1   **Fish-and-Chips Shop with Four Assignments of Lease During a Single Lease Term**

probably seen by buyers as a cash cow with the perks of free food, but is soon realized to be a sweatshop where you literally labor over a hot stove, serving food that you long ago lost the desire to eat, let alone savor. With one fish-and-chips shop in my portfolio, at one stage the business had been sold four times during a single lease term, resulting in four Assignments of Lease. (See Figure 3.1.) I did not mind at all! In my view, there were five parties who were each willingly guaranteeing the payment of rent. We never missed a single dollar of rent payment.

The Tenants Pay the Outgoings

With a residential property, the tenants pay only the rent. There certainly is no suggestion or expectation that the tenant pay the landlord's property taxes, insurance premiums, or maintenance costs. So if a $200,000 home brings in $10,000 in rent, the gross returns are 5 percent, but the net returns will be diminished by the amount of the taxes, insurance, and maintenance.

With commercial leases, however, it is common for tenants to pay not only rent but property taxes, insurance premiums, and maintenance costs as well. These leases are referred to as *triple net*, as the quoted rents are net of those three items, meaning that the tenant has to pay them in addition to the base rent. Consequently, on triple net leases, the gross returns are effectively the net returns.

You could, of course, add the cost of property tax, insurance, and maintenance onto the base rent and come up with a single, all-inclusive rent figure. However, in this case, increases in, say, property taxes for the year would appear to the tenant as an increase in rent. By separating the base rent from the costs, you can keep the base rent amount constant until the next rent review, and any increases in costs will be seen as being beyond your control (as indeed they are).

Insurance premiums are an interesting case. You want to maintain fire insurance, for instance, so that if your building burns down, the insurance company will pay to have the building replaced. Naturally, the tenant pays the premium for this insurance. However, there is another kind of insurance called *consequential loss insurance*. Imagine your building did burn down, and it took four months to rebuild it. You cannot expect the tenants to keep on paying you rent during those four months—they don't have any premises out of which to operate! Consequential loss insurance pays the rent that the tenants cannot pay you as a consequence of the building being rebuilt, thus enabling you to keep up with your mortgage payments and other financial commitments. Guess who pays the premium for the consequential loss insurance? That's right, the tenants do.

Tenants Earn Their Income on Your Premises

While it may seem obvious to mention that commercial tenants earn their income on your premises, the psychological effect of this is enormous. Since they earn their income there, and since they want to increase their income (all other things being equal), two things happen.

Firstly, when something stops working, tenants will not want to call you, wait for you to return the call, arrange a time to meet, agree on what needs to be done, wait for you to hire a tradesman, and then wait for the work to be done. They are operating a business—they want it fixed straight away! Generally they will do it themselves, use an in-house tradesman if their business is large enough, call a friend to fix it, or get it done commercially and pay for it themselves. In general, businesspeople are entrepreneurs. They are go-getters. They want results: Just do it and move on to the next item to be attacked.

This attitude contrasts greatly with that of residential tenants, who often see themselves as the disadvantaged, picked-on victims of overindulgent landlords, and therefore when a faucet leaks, they think nothing of calling the landlord to get it fixed. I have heard of a plumber-tenant who called his landlord when the faucet leaked and, when asked if he could fix it himself (a trivial task for a plumber, after all), replied indignantly, "That is your job. *You* fix it." Obviously, not all residential tenants are quite like that, but there is a definite distinction: Residential tenants tend to leave it to the landlord to fix things, and commercial tenants tend to get the job done themselves. This, of course, is reinforced by what we mentioned in Chapter 2, namely that most commercial lease documents state that the premises must be left in exactly the same condition as when the tenant took on the lease.

The second consequence of tenants earning their income on your premises is that they will always be looking for ways to enhance your property in their quest to earn even more money there. The most obvious example of this is retail stores where, in order to remain fashionable, modern, and appealing, the entire store may need to undergo a major makeover every few years. While such renovations do require your permission under the terms of most commercial leases, they do not require your funding! Here is another example of tenants voluntarily and willingly spending money to enhance their business, but in the process enhancing the building as well.

I have tenants who, of their own free will, completely paint the interiors of their premises every two years, just to keep them looking sparkling (so as to keep attracting customers). Some tenants replace fading awnings regularly, shampoo carpets, and clean windows, not to impress me but to impress their clients. One tenant who operated a restaurant trimmed the neighbor's hedges so that his clients maintained a spectacular view of the bay below. This same tenant put in creative lighting outside and erected a canvas canopy from the road to the front door, all without asking me to foot the bill or even subsidize it.

To understand the significance of commercial tenants making improvements to your property without it costing you anything, compare this scenario with residential tenants. As I write this I am racking my brain to come up with even one instance where a residential tenant offered to or actually improved a house. In all fairness, I do have one tenant in an apartment building who every morning rakes the ground in front of his and other tenants' units, but that is the only example! Furthermore, most residential tenants tend to treat rental properties with some disdain, putting fists through walls, cracking hand-basins, and worse, without even seeming apologetic about it. Such instances of neglect or vandalism (whatever you want to call it) are rare with commercial properties.

So far, we've talked about improvements that don't cost you any money. What about improvements where you are asked to pay?

Landlord Pays for Improvements to Commercial Premises

It is fair to say that if any major improvements are going to be made to a residential property, it will be the landlord who, almost without exception, foots the bill. With commercial real estate, that is not usually the case.

Many commercial leases have a clause stipulating that if a tenant requests major improvements be made, and if the landlord agrees to make and pay for those improvements, then the tenant shall pay extra rent in the amount of x percent of the cost of the improvements. The value of x is usually struck at the time of signing the lease, and will vary depending on prevailing interest rates and market conditions.

With one retail shop, a tenant asked me to demolish the entire front wall, comprising a narrow front door, a relatively small window, and a large brick wall. He wanted it replaced with a glass-curtain front wall with a wide, automatic, sliding glass front door. He was familiar with the lease and knew that he would pay, in this case, 12 percent of the cost of the renovation per annum in the form of extra rent. The renovation bill came in at close to $100,000, and I received an extra $12,000 in rent annually thereafter.

Just how good was this transaction for all parties involved? Well, the tenant was ecstatic, as he didn't have the cash or the inclination to put $100,000 into my building. However, with the $100,000 renovation in place, he felt he could easily generate the extra income from increased retail sales to justify the increased rental. He was very happy.

For my part, on initial inspection, it looks as though I am getting a 12 percent return on an investment of $100,000. Twelve percent is not too bad in anyone's language, but let's look at it a bit more closely.

First, I did spend a real $100,000, but this sum could be capitalized and depreciated (added to the capital basis of the property, and then depreciated for taxation purposes). In this manner, the real cost to me was less than $100,000. Second, by earning an extra $12,000 per annum, the market value of the building increased by over $130,000, since cap rates were around 9 percent at the time (more on cap rates and how they affect values in a later chapter). In other words, by spending $100,000, I increased the value of the building by $130,000. I had just created $30,000 of equity out of thin air!

Third, with an appraisal in hand of $130,000, I easily got a loan for $100,000 at 8 percent interest. Therefore, my net result was that I had a loan for $100,000 secured against an asset that was worth $130,000, costing $8,000 in interest but generating $12,000 in rental. I was making $4,000 a year on money lent by the bank to improve my property, and increased my equity by $30,000. And on top of all that, I had a tenant who thought I was a very obliging landlord for granting his wish to have a fancy shop front.

In this manner, I agree to nearly all my commercial tenants' requests for improvements to their premises. You increase your equity, cash flow, collateral, tax write-offs, and income, all at the same time. It almost seems too good to be true.

Certainty of Collecting Rent

Residential tenants almost always sign the tenancy agreement in their own name. Consequently, they personally pay the rent. Typically, the rent will be in the form of cash, a personal check, or a money order.

Given that you do not want tenants to send cash by mail, for you to receive cash, you have to personally collect it from the tenant (or have your manager do the same). This requires arranging and agreeing on a time to meet, subsequently making the effort to meet, and finally relying on the tenant to have the cash available. Anything can go wrong in this scenario! Either of you may get a flat tire and be late. Maybe the tenant gets to the bank too late and can't withdraw the cash. Maybe he gets to the bank on time but has insufficient funds to withdraw the rent. Maybe he gets mugged on the way home from the bank. Or maybe he claims any of these things happened, and you neither know whether he is telling the truth nor collect your rent.

Similarly, to get a check, you either have to pick it up (and rely on the tenant having sufficient blank checks, a pen that works, being available at the allotted time, and having sufficient funds in the account for the check not to bounce) or have them post it to you, in which case you rely on the envelope being addressed correctly, having the correct postage on it, the check being signed, and once again sufficient funds being in the account to cover the check. If you have been a residential landlord for any time, you know that things do go wrong. Whether these are deliberate ploys on the part of scheming tenants, or innocent foibles of normal humans, collecting rent from residential tenants can be a time-consuming and frustrating exercise.

Commercial tenants are a different breed of payers. First, they seldom sign the lease in their own name—it is usually in the name of their company (often with themselves as guarantors). They understand that rent is one of many fixed operating costs that they are more than willing to pay for the privilege and fun of being in business.

Second, they don't want the bother and hassle of paying you in cash, or even by check. Most commercial rents are paid by automatic bank transfers every month. As of this writing, all of my commercial tenants around the world, with the exception of two newcomers whom we are in the process of converting, pay by automatic bank transfer. It is easier not only for us but for them, too.

Look at it this way. With residential tenants paying by cash, check, or money order, for the rent to be paid, an entire sequence of events needs to take place: a combination of withdrawing cash, setting up a meeting, being present at that meeting, having blank checks, having a pen that works, and so forth. If any crucial step is missed, the rent will not be paid. This can happen when the tenant is out of town on vacation, when you or your property manager is on vacation, when the allotted meeting day is a public holiday, when the tenant is in the hospital visiting a sick relative, or when they (or you!) simply forget something.

Conversely, with commercial tenants paying by automatic bank transfer, the default condition is that the rent is paid every month. In order for the rent *not* to be paid, action must be taken, such as contacting the bank to stop the payment for that month or from then on. In other words, wherever you are, and wherever the tenant is, and whether either of you has a pen that works, blank checks, flat tires, bank holidays, or whatever, the rent will be paid unless an order is given to stop payment.

Upward-Only Rent Reviews

We all know that markets go up, and markets come down. Whether we are talking about the price of gas, commodities, stocks, coffee beans, houses, commercial buildings, or residential rentals, we have all experienced upward and downward price movements, even if the long-term underlying trend is upwards.

However, while residential rentals can decline in a down market, commercial rentals tend not to, for the simple reason that most commercial leases have what is known as an "upward-only rent review" clause in them. This clause means exactly what it says, namely that with a rent review, the rent may stay the same or it may go up, but it will not go down.

Initially, this clause may seem to unfairly favor the landlord. The argument against this clause goes along these lines: If the economy is strong, and everything is going up in price, it is perhaps reasonable that commercial rents go up, but if the economy is in decline and everything is going down, commercial rents should decline as well.

While on the surface this seems like a sensible argument, the reality is that an upward-only rent review clause enables commercial landlords to offer a lower base rental than they otherwise would be able to if they had to build in a buffer should rents decline. The ensuing effect of this is that it provides stability to the commercial rental market.

In some parts of the world this clause is called a *ratchet clause*. Please note that *ratchet* is one word—many people pronounce it as though it were two!

Government Interference

Most countries have very detailed and specific laws governing how residential real estate is rented. Some laws are probably reasonable, such as the requirement to give a tenant 24 hours notice of intent to inspect a property. Other laws totally baffle me, though, such as the law that prevents a law-abiding landlord from taking any action whatsoever against a tenant who, without warning, fails to pay his rent and continues not to pay for up to 90 days, as in California, for instance. Some of these tenants know the rules so well that they stay as long as they possibly can in one rental property (not paying the rent) before moving on to their next victim. In parts of Europe, if squatters are not evicted within a certain short time frame, it becomes impossible to evict them at all or to charge them rent. What an incentive to become a squatter!

I can think of no justification whatsoever for some of these bizarre laws, although I believe I can probably explain them on the basis that there are more tenant voters than landlord voters in any election.

Having said all that, when it comes to commercial real estate, there does not seem to be anywhere near as much interference by the government. If a commercial tenant does not pay his rent, the landlord has about as much power for remedial action as does a car leasing company dealing with nonpayment (repossess the car) or a hotel dealing with a nonpaying guest (toss him out and retain something as collateral to ensure the bill is paid). After all, when you sign a contract to lease a car or occupy a hotel room, you agree to receive the use of the goods in exchange for money; if you fail to meet your financial obligations, you should lose the use of the goods! Why governments let residential tenants get away with the analogous failure to pay rent baffles me. Fortunately, they have not yet legislated that commercial tenants can get away with nonpayment. That is another big advantage of commercial real estate.

To put it another way, imagine a friendly entrepreneur rents both his residential accommodation and his place of work, be it retail space, offices, or whatever. And imagine that he does not have sufficient funds to pay both his residential and commercial rent. I would predict that he will pay the commercial rent long before he even thinks of paying the residential rent, for the simple reason that the repercussions of not paying the commercial rent are far more severe.

Management Overhead

We have already seen how residential tenants will phone you about the most trivial problems, whereas commercial tenants tend to look after things themselves. We have seen how commercial tenants sign up for long-term leases, resulting in lower tenant turnover. We have seen how collecting rent from residential tenants can be a nightmare, whereas collecting rent from commercial tenants in general is a breeze.

The management overhead of commercial real estate is trivial compared with that of residential real estate. To be sure, owning commercial real estate does require some management. You have to keep track of when leases expire and when rent reviews are due. You must have systems in place to maintain the properties, deal with unexpected events, ensure rents are paid, and pay your own related bills such as property taxes. However, managing residential real estate is, for all the reasons we've already discussed, a much more time-consuming exercise.

To illustrate the difference, for all the residential properties that I still have in my portfolio, I have property managers looking after them. It is simply too time consuming and difficult to manage residential properties in my own area, and virtually impossible to manage them from afar. By contrast, I have numerous commercial buildings not under property management for the simple reason that they require so little management that it would be silly to give up, say, 5 percent of the rent roll (as a management fee) to have a property manager field three phone calls a year and write a rent review letter every two years.

CHAPTER 4

The Downside of Commercial Real Estate

Whenever I speak in public about commercial real estate and solicit advantages over residential real estate from the audience, I always get disgruntled naysayers trying to prove me wrong by pointing out *disadvantages*. So, in the interest of fairness and balance, let's review these perceived disadvantages, and then I will give my take on them.

Much More Difficult to Acquire Commercial Tenants

When you have a rental house that has been vacant for more than a month or so, there is only one reason why that house has not been tenanted. It is not because the color of the carpet in the master bedroom is wrong, or because the aspect of the kitchen window relative to where the sun rises in winter is wrong, or because the shower has the wrong showerhead. The only reason why the property is not tenanted is because the rent is too high. Drop the rent by 10 or 15 percent, or, if need be, by 20 percent, and you will more than likely find a tenant.

By contrast, when you have a commercial property that has been vacant for even a day, the fact that there is no tenant may have very little to do with the rental level. Most commercial properties are suited to a specific and narrow class of activities, and you cannot fit just any commercial operation into the premises. For instance, a vacant bottling plant will have no appeal to a shoe retailer, a vacant retail shop will have no appeal to a car-painting operation, and a property designed for car painting will have no appeal for someone operating an ice-cream parlor.

In this sense, it can be much more difficult to secure a commercial tenant for a vacant commercial property than to secure a residential tenant for a house. This is, after all, one of the prime reasons investors cite as to why they are reluctant to get into commercial real estate. Commercial premises can be vacant for months or even years at a time. Hold that thought.

Banks Will Lend a Smaller Proportion of a Commercial Property

With residential property, banks are willing to lend a large proportion of the purchase price. The loan-to-value ratio (LTV) can be as high as 80 percent without the banks requiring you to purchase mortgage insurance, and if you do get mortgage insurance, they are willing to go to 90, 95, or even 100 percent. Recently it was possible to get a mortgage with an LTV of 125 percent—fully 25 percent more than the house is costing you.

When it comes to commercial real estate, however, banks appear to be far more conservative and often have LTV limits of 50, 60, or in some exceptional cases 70 percent. The net result is the perception among the masses that, whereas you can buy a house with 10 percent down, or even 5 percent down, or even with nothing down, when it comes to commercial property, you need to have huge reserves of cash.

So far, in the disadvantage list for commercial property, we have seen that it can be very difficult to secure a tenant for commercial premises, and that banks are willing to lend a much smaller proportion of the value of a commercial property than of a residential property. These two disadvantages seem to be insurmountable, and I am sure they have put legions of otherwise enthusiastic investors off the idea of delving into commercial real estate.

To figure out how we are going to overcome these seemingly insurmountable problems, we need to understand a supremely important difference between residential and commercial real estate, one that is so fundamental and yet so easy to miss that we devote an entire chapter to it.

CHAPTER 5

The True Value of Real Estate

In determining the value of a residential property, a lot of factors are taken into account. Size, age, condition; number of bedrooms and bathrooms; views; susceptibility to wind, flooding, and hurricanes; proximity to desired services such as shops; close proximity to undesired features such as freeways; crime statistics; school district; and zoning restrictions all play a role in determining the ultimate value.

Having said all that, however, a four-bedroom, three-bathroom house that is 12 years old and in great condition will sell for essentially the same price as a similar four-bedroom, three-bathroom house that is also 12 years old and in great condition nearby.

Furthermore, the value of that house will not be affected by whether the house is tenanted. You could even argue that the value of the house might be a bit less if it *is* tenanted, on the basis that if the buyer wants to occupy it, he must first get rid of the tenant, something that may not be easy to do in many jurisdictions. However, in general, a four-bedroom, three-bathroom house in that area with all those features is worth the same as any similar house, tenanted or not.

That brings us to our first formula, which will start to put what we have said into perspective:

$$\text{Return} = \frac{\text{Rental Income}}{\text{Purchase Price}}$$

This formula simply says that the returns we can expect from a residential property will be the rental income divided by the purchase price. Using our example from the Chapter 3, if the house costs $200,000 to buy, and the rental income is $10,000 per annum, then the return on investment (ROI) is 5 percent ($10,000/$200,000).

Now ask yourself, what determines the rental income for this house? Can the landlord dictate what that rent will be? Of course not! The market determines the rent. If the landlord charges too much, the tenants will leave in favor of a similar house at a cheaper rent. So the rental income is determined by the market.

What about the purchase price? Can the landlord choose his own purchase price? Of course not! The purchase price is also determined by the market. A buyer might find a bargain, but in general he will have to pay a fair market price for the house.

Consequently, the return our residential investor can expect to get from this or any other property is entirely determined by the market. The return is the quotient of one market-determined factor (the rental income) divided by another market-determined factor (the purchase price). There is very little our residential investor can do, using his creativity, talents, or skills, to improve his returns.

Commercial property is an entirely different beast. With commercial real estate, the following formula applies:

$$\text{Property Value} = \frac{\text{Rental Income}}{\text{Capitalization Rate}}$$

This formula says that the value of the real estate is simply the rental that it generates, divided by the applicable capitalization rate. What is the capitalization rate? The *capitalization rate*, generally referred to as the *cap rate*, is the rate at which you capitalize the rental income to arrive at the capital value.

Assume for a moment that investors will only buy an investment if they can get a 10 percent return on their capital every year. In other words, if they invest $1 million, they want to get $100,000 return every year, or they are not interested.

Now assume an investor is looking at buying a property, and all he knows is that the property generates $100,000 per annum. It doesn't even matter what was paid for it originally. What would he be willing to pay for this investment? If he wants to see a 10 percent return, then he should not offer more than $1 million for it.

Can our commercial real estate investor decide what cap rates apply to his building? Of course not! Cap rates are determined by the market. In essence, the market cap rate for a particular building in a particular area is the average of all the ROIs that similar buildings in that area have been selling at. So, if the last 10 sales all showed an ROI of 10 percent, then the market cap rate is 10 percent.

Thus, if market cap rates are 10 percent, and you find a building for sale with an ROI of only 8 percent, then all other things being equal, this is not a good investment, as you could get a higher return elsewhere. Conversely, if market cap rates are 10 percent, and you find a building for sale with an ROI of 13 percent, then all other things being equal, this is a good investment, as you are getting a higher return than the market average.

Another way of looking at it is that if market cap rates are 10 percent, and you can buy a property with an ROI of 13 percent, it is a good deal because in theory you should be able to turn around and sell that building at a cap rate of 10 percent. For instance, assuming a building has a rental income of $100,000, if you can buy this building at $769,230 (a 13 percent return), it is a good deal because you should be able to sell it (should you be so inclined) for $1 million (a 10 percent return). Even if you do not sell this building, it is still worth $1 million (because your rental income is $100,000 and market cap rates are 10 percent), and you are only paying $769,230 for it, so you have instant equity.

Now you must realize that cap rates are not the same everywhere and for all time. Investors covet real estate on Wall Street in New York, because you will always be able to find tenants willing to pay a high rent just to be able to boast that their offices are on the most famous street in the financial capital of the world. Cap rates on Wall Street are typically around 5 percent, meaning that given a rental income of $100,000, an investor would be willing to pay $2 million ($100,000 divided by 5 percent).

Conversely, in some small town in the middle of nowhere, cap rates might be 25 percent per annum, meaning investors would need to see a return of 25 percent before placing their money in a town with not nearly as much appeal as Wall Street in New York. In this case, a rental income of $100,000 would mean the building is worth only $400,000 ($100,000 divided by 25 percent).

If you are new to this concept of cap rates, it may all seem a bit confusing, especially since a low cap rate equates to a high capital value, and a high cap rate equates to a relatively low capital value. Persevere, as what we are discussing here will form the basis of your commercial real estate success.

Let's refer once again to our formula for commercial real estate:

$$\text{Property Value} = \frac{\text{Rental Income}}{\text{Cap Rate}}$$

It should be obvious that, based on this formula, there are only two ways to increase the property value. One is to increase the rental income. The other is to lower the cap rate.

Increasing the income is a great game to play as there are so many ways of doing it—so many that we devote an entire chapter to it (see Chapter 8). The point that you should remember, however, which should keep you awake at night with excitement, is the fact that if you are creative and manage to double the income generated by a commercial property, the value of that property essentially doubles.

Try that with residential real estate! Even if you managed to double the rental on a home from $1,000 a month to $2,000 a month—or, conversely, if you lost the tenant and the rental income went to zero—you would still be able to sell the house for about the same price, because the value of a house is determined by what other houses of similar size, features, age, condition, and aspect command. With houses, as we have seen, the rental income is determined by the market, and the value of the house is determined by the market. With commercial real estate, the cap rate is determined by the market, but the value of a property is the rental income divided by the cap rate—in other words, the value of a commercial property is in direct proportion to the income it generates. When you double the income, you essentially double the value. What a recipe for fortune!

The second way to increase the value of a building is to wait for cap rates to fall. Cap rates do not remain static. In general, when the market is strong, cap rates fall (since investors are willing to accept lower returns in a strong market). Conversely, when the market is weakening, cap rates rise (as investors want higher returns to compensate for the increasing risk of investing).

Assume a building has $100,000 of income, and you bought it for $1 million at a time when the market cap rate for buildings like yours was 10 percent. In this case, you would have bought it at its prevailing market value ($100,000 divided by 10 percent). If the market is strengthening, and cap rates fall to, say, 8 percent, then without even changing the rental income, painting the building, or doing anything else, the value of your building will have risen to $1.25 million ($100,000 divided by 8 percent).

Realize that we cannot force the cap rate to go lower (or higher), as it is determined by the market. However, if the market is strong, cap rates do tend to fall, and if the market is weak, cap rates tend to rise.

Most people get confused with the concept of cap rates because real estate agents freely use the term to refer to the return on a building. For instance, an agent may tell you that a property is "selling at a cap rate of 11 percent." This, of course, has little meaning until you know what market cap rates for similar buildings in the same area are. After all, if market cap rates were 7 percent, and you were offered this building at 11 percent, you would probably have a good deal; whereas if market cap rates were 15 percent, then a building returning 11 percent would look like a lousy deal—and yet in both cases, the return was the same 11 percent.

To say a building is "selling at a cap rate of 11 percent" may not be entirely incorrect, but I feel it is misleading at best. They are saying that the cap rate is the rental income divided by their asking price, and it therefore hides how the asking price came about. If instead we say "the building is offered at a return of 11 percent," then at least it may give some people the sense to find out what market cap rates are.

Therefore, I prefer you to think in terms of "this property is being offered with a return of 11 percent in a market where prevailing cap rates are 10 percent." Use the term *return* (or *return on investment*, or *ROI*) to describe what the returns are when you are presented with a given rental income and a given purchase price. Use the term *cap rate* when you want to extrapolate what a property is worth given a certain income. Thinking in this way will help you make millions in commercial real estate, as you will see.

So, just to reiterate, the return on an investment is the income divided by the purchase price. The cap rate is the rate at which you capitalize the income on a commercial property to arrive at the property value. Cap rates are entirely determined by the market.

CHAPTER 6

How to Overcome the Disadvantages of Commercial Real Estate

So far we have discovered that commercial real estate has some tremendous advantages over residential real estate. Just to summarize, with commercial real estate, you have the following eight advantages:

1. Leases are longer term.

2. You have assignment-of-lease protection.

3. The tenants pay the outgoings.

4. The tenants renovate the building at their cost.

5. When you pay for a renovation, the tenants pay you an increased rent.

6. The tenants earn their income on your property.

7. There is less government interference.

8. You have reduced management overhead.

However, in Chapter 4, we discovered two major disadvantages of commercial real estate:

1. It is generally much harder to find a tenant for a commercial property.

2. Banks tend to offer a much lower loan to value (LTV) on commercial real estate, meaning you need a higher proportion of the purchase price in cash.

Have I skillfully deflected us from addressing these disadvantages by introducing the concept of cap rates in the preceding chapter? No, on the contrary, we needed to understand cap rates to appreciate how you can overcome these apparent disadvantages.

The reason a house is worth about the same vacant as it is when tenanted is precisely because it is relatively easy to find a tenant for any house. Conversely, the reason why a commercial property is worth so little vacant, and so much when tenanted, is because it can be relatively difficult to attract a tenant to a commercial building.

The increase in value of a commercial building when you find a tenant is a reward for the skill, experience, and tenacity that you applied in attracting a tenant. Notice I did not include the word *luck* in the list of attributes that help you attract a tenant. Sure, you may get lucky every now and then and stumble upon a tenant, but successful commercial real estate investors have mastered the art of attracting tenants.

When I was just starting out in real estate, I kept thinking about the simple formula that property value equals rental income divided by cap rate. Compared with the formulae that I had worked with earning a PhD in electrical engineering, this one was trivial. And yet I knew that embedded in it was a route to vast wealth. I kept thinking that if one could devise a methodology for consistently finding tenants for vacant commercial properties, then the values of those properties would escalate tremendously.

I looked at what other people were doing to attract tenants. Almost without exception, landlords simply placed a classified advertisement in the local newspaper and then waited for masses of potential tenants to beat a path to their door, holding wads of cash and offering far more than the asking rent. Of course, no such thing eventuated, and the clueless landlords simply placed another advertisement the following week and repeated their optimistic waiting game. If it took a year to attract a tenant, then that was simply an indication of how tough the market was.

I decided from day one that I was not going to be held hostage by the limited power of a newspaper advertisement to find a tenant for me. The evidence clearly showed that this was not a smart way of operating. So, with little experience in real estate, a good dose of common sense, and huge amounts of enthusiasm, I set about to create my own universe, one where there was an abundant supply of tenants.

These ideas have worked so well that I still apply them today, and furthermore, I can boast a full house in my entire global portfolio. Admittedly, some properties are in markets where any vacant space gets snapped up quickly, but others are in markets where there are huge vacancies, and yet I still have a full house.

In Chapter 7 I share just how we find tenants, and then I devote a chapter to how to increase rental rates even further. These two concepts will help you unleash the incredible wealth-building power of commercial real estate investing.

How to Attract a Tenant

We tend to live in a very self-centered society, where the focus is on "me." "What's in it for me?" is a common catch-phrase, and people tend to write, "*I* would like to express my thanks for . . ." instead of simply "Thank *you* for . . ." In English, unlike many other languages, we even write *I* with a capital letter and *you* with a small letter. As a spin-off of this self-centeredness, if we cannot imagine doing something, we have difficulty imagining anyone else doing it.

Who Wants to Run a Funeral Business?

When I first came across the funeral parlor mentioned in Chapter 3, it was vacant and the owner had been trying to sell it for some three years. No one could imagine owning it, as they couldn't imagine anyone wanting to be the tenant. After all, do you know what goes on inside a funeral parlor? Doesn't really bear thinking about, does it? And yet, funeral parlors are not exactly a dying industry, if you will excuse the pun.

Nonetheless, this property had been vacant for some time, and when a property has been on the market for a long time, it is said to go "stale." Investors tend to think, "Wow, no one else has bought this property in all the three years that it has been on the market, and I am sure there must be some very smart investors who have looked at it in that time, so if they rejected it, then surely I would have to be a big fool to go and buy it, so I, too, will pass on it."

As far as I could tell, the listing agents had only advertised this property in the local newspaper. What is more, the property had been put up for auction some months prior, but got passed in as bids failed to meet the reserve price of $195,000.

What can we conclude so far? First, that there was not a strong demand for funeral homes, and second, that the minimum price we would have to pay was $195,000, as that was the reserve price at the auction, right?

Wrong! You cannot conclude that there was a low demand for funeral homes when the seller had only advertised locally, three years on the market notwithstanding. Second, the auction may have had a reserve price of $195,000, but long after the auction and its disappointing result, the seller may have been ready to quit at a lower price.

What did I do? I employed someone at $8 an hour to phone funeral operators in other cities, starting with those close by and slowly fanning out, to find out if they were interested in expanding into this town. (In case you think $8 an hour is cheap, this was nearly 20 years ago and it was a good hourly rate at the time.)

Nowadays a task like this is much easier, as you can use the Internet to find numbers to call. Back then we used stacks of Yellow Pages books from other areas, and a lot of directory assistance calls, to track down other funeral operators.

My assistant was on the phone for a full two days. Many of our phone calls were not welcomed, with gruff people telling us that they had better things to do than to entertain the idea of expanding into another town. A couple of people were downright rude, and some were amused. Some simply hung up on us. Oh, and I nearly forgot to mention, one said he was extremely interested in expanding into this town, as he operated a thriving funeral business in a town about 80 miles away, and thought (it sounds terrible) that he could get economies of scale on his operation.

The first thing I did is tell him that there was a vacant funeral parlor for sale, and if he wanted to buy it I could give him the details. Now, given that I wanted to buy the building myself, why on earth would I offer it to him?

The answer is simple. I knew that, in all probability, he had no interest in owning the building. However, what if he did? Imagine if he became the tenant, and then found out that I had just bought the building. The last thing you want is a tenant who begrudges the fact that the only reason you are his landlord is because you beat him to buying the building. And if you are thinking, "Well that would be his tough luck, he signed the lease, so stuff him!" you are missing a big point about landlord-tenant relations that we cover later. As it turned out, he was not interested in owning the building. He said, "I know how to run funerals, not properties. I don't want to be my own landlord. But if you buy the building, I will rent it from you."

So, having dismissed the suggestion that he buy the property, we met to inspect the building and work out initial rent and other details. He then signed a "Heads of Agreement," where, subject to my buying the property, he would become the tenant on a 10-plus-10 year lease.

Note that I still had not bought the building at that point! (See Figure 7.1.) I didn't want to take the risk of buying a funeral parlor and then not having a tenant for it. So I set out to find a tenant first. Nothing wrong with that!

Armed with my Heads of Agreement, which guaranteed I would receive $30,000 a year in rent, and knowing that market cap rates were hovering around 12 percent, I knew that the building should be worth around $250,000 ($30,000 divided by 12 percent). So here was an interesting anomaly: To me, with a tenant in

Figure 7.1   **Part of the Funeral Parlor Buildings**

tow, the building was worth a lot more than it was to the seller, who still had a vacant building. In fact, I ended up buying the building for $170,000. The difference between the purchase price and the $250,000 value was effectively created by employing someone for two days at $8 an hour to find a tenant. That's a profit of $80,000 (tax free if I don't sell) for an investment of only $128 (tax deductible!)—plus I get a lifetime of passive income from the property, along with increasing rents, capital values, collateral, and equity.

And all of this was possible because I realized that, unlike residential real estate, where a building is worth about the same whether it is tenanted or not, with commercial real estate, a tenanted building is worth a lot more than that same building vacant. Or, going back to our formula:

$$\text{Property Value} = \frac{\text{Rental Income}}{\text{Cap Rate}}$$

I could not affect the cap rate, which was around 12 percent at the time. But I did affect the rental income and, as a consequence, the property value.

In case you are wondering why the property did not sell for $1 or even nothing, there are a number of factors that prevented that. First, there is of course some residual land value and some residual building value, even if the premises are vacant. Second, in this case, the seller was willing to sign a 12-year lease to occupy a small portion (800 square feet) of a second building, providing some rental income that could still be capped out at 12 percent. Third, the property included a two-story, triple-brick, four-bedroom house, which added to the inherent value.

Finding a Tenant for a Warehouse in an Oversupplied Market

Another category of commercial real estate that most landlords find difficult to fill is the simple warehouse. Imagine you have a vacant warehouse in a suburb where there are vacant warehouses everywhere. What would you do? You could call me and offer me 50 percent of the property if I found a tenant. I know I would find one quickly.

You might also try this: Obtain, create, make, beg, or cajole someone into giving you a list of all warehouse operators in the vicinity. You could use the Yellow Pages, inquire at the Chamber of Commerce, or use the Internet. Then phone (or employ someone else to phone) each warehouse operator in turn, first those within half a mile of your premises, then within one mile, and so on. Imagine you have a vacant 20,000-square-foot warehouse. The conversation would go something like this:

> You: "I understand you have a warehouse on Jackson Avenue."
>
> Them: "That's right, so what?"
>
> You: "Do you mind me asking how much area you rent?"
>
> Them: "We have about 12,000 square feet. Why?"
>
> You: "Well, we were wondering if you were expanding and needing more space, as we have a 20,000-square-foot warehouse nearby."
>
> Them: "Nope, but thanks for asking."
>
> Or:

"Get lost and don't ever dare call me again."

Or:

"Actually we might be, let me ask my boss."

Or:

"Yes, we desperately need more space! Thank God you called—we haven't had time to look for new premises."

There are, of course, many other possible answers. The point is, you just want to keep phoning warehouse tenants until you find one who wants to consider your space.

Now, not all existing warehouses will be smaller than the one you have. If they have a larger warehouse, the conversation may go like this:

You: "I understand you have a warehouse on Jackson Avenue."

Them: "That's right, so what?"

You: "Do you mind me asking how much area you rent?"

Them: "We have about 28,000 square feet. Why?"

You: "Well, we were wondering if you were consolidating and/or downsizing and needing less space, as we have a 20,000-square-foot warehouse nearby."

Them: "Nope, but thanks for asking."

Or:

"Get lost and don't ever dare call me again."

Or:

"Actually we might be, let me ask my boss."

Or:

> "Yes, we desperately need less space. Thank God you called—we haven't had time to look for new premises."

And what about (it *will* happen!) if they already have exactly 20,000 square feet? Ask them if they are happy, and if not, then you have a chance to sway them on factors other than rental area.

Most people are put off making calls like this, as they cannot stand the rejection. But remember that Thomas Edison tried more than 1,000 ways to make a light bulb before he found one that worked. Each time a new idea did not work, he didn't wallow in despair and berate himself for being a hopeless inventor. Rather, as he later put it, he found more than 1,000 successful ways of not making a light bulb.

In a similar vein, don't let your mood or self-esteem be affected by 50 people telling you they do not want to rent your 20,000-square-foot warehouse. You only need one to say yes, and bingo! You have an efficient and easy-to-manage investment that will feed you for the rest of your life if you are smart enough never to sell.

Based on the law of averages, if you make enough phone calls, you will get people agreeing at least to have a look at your warehouse. What should you do next—just stand there chewing gum, hoping that a prospective tenant coming to have a look will sign the lease on the spot and start throwing money at you? No, you have to be more creative than that. Watch less television, read fewer trash magazines, spend less time with indulgent friends, and start to *think*!

In general, who will come to inspect your warehouse? Will it be the chairman of the board of directors? Ridiculous! Will it be the CFO at national headquarters? No, of course not! Will it be the president of the company? No, don't be silly. Will it be the janitor who will have to keep the warehouse clean? Again, no. Will it be the tea and coffee person who will satisfy everyone's craving for caffeine? No! It will in nearly all cases be the warehouse manager—the person who will oversee the operation at the warehouse for the company, and therefore the person who will occupy the manager's office. So how do you get him to say yes to your warehouse when there are dozens on the market for miles around?

The way to have your warehouse tenanted even in a high-vacancy market is simple. Spend $10,000 making the manager's office the most salubrious office that the average manager has ever seen. Replace the windows with dual-pane or double-glazed windows to keep out noise and extreme temperatures. Put in a commercial grade carpet—most warehouse manager's offices have either concrete or linoleum on the floor. Replace unappealing fluorescent tube lights with halogen spotlights. Put in a bar and refrigerator, and let the manager's imagination run rife with what he may keep in there for the weekly end-of-week celebration. Put in an espresso machine in case the manager likes coffee. Install a sound system. Next (I am not kidding) mount a large LCD or plasma screen on the wall opposite his desk, and hook it up to nine security cameras strategically mounted around and inside the premises. He will be able to justify his choice of warehouse to his bosses on this one feature alone (security for the premises and the company's stock, and monitoring of the performance of the workers). And what if, in addition to the images of security cameras, the screen is capable of displaying DVDs? Great! Install a DVD player as well, and mention that the player is useful for company training videos (he may not think that's what he'll use if for, but you will have given him a line he can use with his bosses).

Next, put in brand-new and stately furniture, including a large office desk and a reclining leather office chair. Add a good-quality phone, some artwork, and a high-security or even electronic lock on the door, and you have created something that will be so tempting to any warehouse manager that you will be shaking your head in disbelief that you didn't implement these things before.

We are all human beings, and we all succumb to temptation. You have to understand the psyche of a warehouse manager, who works every day, week in, week out, at a warehouse. Not a fancy retail shop where he would get to meet all manner of interesting people (well, so it seems to the warehouse manager), but people in overalls doing the work that gets done in warehouses. In all honesty, any one of the ideas above may clinch the tenant, but why not go for broke? After all, the total cost of these modifications isn't that great. In fact, I think you would be hard-pressed to spend $10,000 in total, with DVD players costing less than $50, espresso machines $30, and huge LCD screens costing under $1,000 and plummeting further by the day.

At a market rental of, say, $10 per square foot (psf), a 20,000-square-foot warehouse is worth $200,000 a year. Surely $10,000 spent titivating the manager's office is cheap if it helps you secure a tenant even one month sooner than you otherwise would have, let alone if you get the tenant a year or two earlier.

This is what taking initiative is all about! And it beats placing an advertisement in the local newspaper week after week, hoping to secure a tenant for a nondescript warehouse in a sea of similarly nondescript warehouses.

The Power of the Internet

While phoning around is a very efficient way to attract prospective tenants who are already somewhat prequalified (in the preceding example, they already rent a warehouse), I would not rely on that method alone, just as I think it is silly to rely on newspaper advertisements alone. Think about it—newspapers are going out of fashion, as people's attention and quest for news is being hijacked by the Internet; by instant, live coverage on an ever-expanding network of cable channels; by RSS feeds, blogs, pod-casts, and instant notification services by video on your cell phone over 3G networks. I, for one, have not subscribed to a newspaper in years, preferring the ease of browsing, search capabilities, paperless storage of articles of interest, and the ability to retrieve anything I have decided to archive from any computer in the world. For similar reasons, many potential tenants may likewise not see your advertisement for space for rent in the local newspaper.

How do you overcome the problem of dwindling subscribers to newspapers? Join the masses! If people are spending so much time on the Internet, advertise on the Internet. The phenomenal rise in popularity of web sites such as Craig's List (www.craigslist.com) is mind-boggling enough from an anthropological point of view, but it also tells you what you should be doing: Advertise on them!

I think back to the time when we used to advertise exclusively in newspapers (in the pre-Internet age). You had to establish an account with the newspaper—otherwise they would not carry your advertisement. To establish an account, you had to go through hoops to prove you were real and creditworthy and not about to place an ad for space in a commercial building and then not pay the cost of the ad. Of course if you wanted to advertise in two newspapers, then you had to establish accounts at both. You had to create the copy and, in some cases, the layout, a minimum number of days before the advertisement was going to appear. The forward planning required, and the waiting, let alone the cost, was substantial.

Today, you can place an advertisement on Craigslist.com or any number of other sites, and potentially get a response the same day. It doesn't always happen that way, but we advertised for a tenant for a retail property on various sites one day, and had a tenant signed up that night. The fact that most of these sites are free is beside the point—I would be happy to pay a lot of money to secure a $200,000-a-year tenant, but if you can get one quickly *and* free, why not?

Another way of embracing the Internet is to establish a web site specifically for your vacant spaces. Include a colorful and accurate write-up. Put in photos—not one or two, and not photos the size of postage stamps, but 10 or even 30 or more photos that can be enlarged on a computer to give the reader a great idea of what the premises are like. Include, as appropriate, foot-traffic counts, proximity to freeways, other shops in the vicinity, views—anything that can make a prospective tenant feel inclined to check out your property. If it is a retail site that you are trying to lease out, consider putting a webcam on-site to show prospective tenants how many potential customers are walking by at the very moment that the prospective tenant is looking at your web site.

Many Prospective Tenants Know Your Building

Often, prospective tenants already know about your premises before you even begin to advertise. I once bought a retail center that included a butcher shop. One day I got a call from a woman who asked if she could lease my premises from me. I politely told her that I had a full house, but that I was willing to take down her details in case something came up. She responded with amusement that I certainly did not have a full house, unless I considered the 3 million flies in the closed-down butcher shop tenants. An inspection revealed that she was right—the butcher had simply shut down his shop, and left his meat behind to rot, attracting the aforementioned flies.

The butcher leaving the way he did turned out to be fortuitous for me. The caller signed up for a 12-year lease, and converted the premises from a butcher shop—a dying operation in the face of competition from aggressively priced and convenient supermarkets—to a gourmet delicatessen. (See Figure 7.2.) As part of this conversion, she spent $30,000 of her own money renovating my premises. No doubt she did this with self-interest in mind, and I am sure it paid off for her, as she subsequently sold the business for a handsome profit. However, for my part, I still own the premises, and still have the value of the $30,000 she spent on my building. In addition, as we have already seen, when she sold the business and assigned the lease (with my permission), I had the added benefit of a second person lining up to pay the rent should the first default.

This woman called me, however, because she had seen the premises vacant. I believe that most prospective tenants live, work, or operate in the general vicinity of your property. So I got to thinking, why do real estate agents who advertise commercial real estate for lease limit themselves to a small "For Lease" sign the size of a standard sheet of paper? Why not go large?

Here is what I do, and I recommend you do the same. Get a huge—10 foot by 20 foot, or even larger—banner made out of

Figure 7.2 **Butcher Shop Turned Delicatessen**

durable canvas, with the words "For Lease" up top, and your phone number down below. If you have a URL specifically for your vacant premises, include the web address. Do not clutter the banner with extraneous details about the property—it only makes the text more difficult to read, and anyway, people are not going to stop driving on the freeway to read your banner thesis. Besides, if all you have is "For Lease" and a phone number and web address, then you can use the sign again and again on other buildings.

Surprisingly, the cost of a banner sign like this is not thousands of dollars. Even if it was, I would say get half a dozen made because, again, the value of getting even one tenant even one month earlier than you otherwise would is tremendous. However, you can get these banners made, using computer etching, for around $100. Hang one on every vacant building you have. If the building faces two streets, hang one on each side. The results will make you a convert.

Not everything has to be electronic or computer-etched on canvas. Create a flier of your vacant premises, make several hundred copies (preferably in color), and have them delivered within a mile or so of the premises. You will be surprised how often you will find a tenant this way. The convenience store operator who reads your flier happens to have a cousin who needs space for his car-painting shop. The parking lot owner wants covered parking for long-term clients. The baker's in-laws need a retail shop and warehouse for their European specialty food importing business.

Visit the local chamber of commerce. Depending on where you live, it may be actively involved with start-up businesses, and you may be able to advertise your vacant space on its notice board or web site. Similarly, visit the local Better Business Bureau, Council Initiative for Economic Development (or variations on this theme), or retailers' association.

Engage a Real Estate Firm or Property Management Company to Find a Tenant

Real estate agents or property managers can be great sources of tenants. The big advantage is that often they have a list of prospective tenants on their books who are looking for specific kinds of real estate. This list of tenants can be filtered on the basis of the size of premises they are seeking, the geographic area, the type of premises, and features they want to see included or excluded.

The commensurate disadvantage of using agents or a management company is that they will charge a fee for finding a tenant, the amount of which varies from region to region. In the United States it is common for an agent or broker who brings you a tenant to receive a percentage of the annual rent for the duration of the lease—and 6 percent per year for a 10-year lease can add up! However, it may be well worthwhile if the alternative is not to have a tenant.

In any case, before signing a leasing agreement with a firm, make sure you understand exactly what the fee structure is and what they will do to attract a tenant. Also, make sure you understand whether they still get a fee if you should manage to secure a tenant through your own efforts.

Wait for (or Cause) a Zone Change

The kinds of activities that may be conducted at a particular property location are usually determined by what is, in most parts of the world, called the *zoning*. Zoning regulations are usually determined by local councils. You cannot build apartments, let alone commercial premises, where the zoning stipulates that only single-family residences may be erected. Similarly, you may not be able to construct a 10-story office tower in an area zoned for retail space. Zoning laws can be very complex, and even minor infringements can cause you a lot of trouble. Having said that, just because a property has a particular zoning allocated to it does not mean it has to stay that way forever.

Cities are in a constant state of evolution and growth, and accordingly, zoning designations are continually being updated, modified, and amended. There are two mechanisms to benefit from the fact that zoning designations change from time to time.

One method is to attend public council meetings where zoning changes are tabled, discussed, debated, and decided. If, for instance, you find out that a particular street in the downtown part of your city will have its zoning changed from residential to commercial, then it stands to reason that you can buy some of those homes, wait for the zone change to take effect, and then rent the properties out, not as residences, but as professional offices at a much higher rental rate.

Generally, houses undergoing a zone change can be bought relatively cheaply because, notwithstanding the fact that the council meetings are public, most people simply do not attend them, send someone to attend on their behalf, or bother to read the reports (usually available online) as to what went on at the meetings. You can get insider information and legally use it to make a fortune. I find it ironic that the information that can make you a fortune is publicly available, and yet few people bother to find out about it. What is more, if you do go to the bother to find out, and you subsequently act on that information to make a small fortune, there are no legal repercussions of doing so—you are perfectly within your rights. This contrasts dramatically with the stock market, where any form of insider trading is frowned upon, and people end up going to jail. I much prefer working in an industry where there are no repercussions to using publicly available information, rather than an industry where, if I use something I hear to make a profit, I risk going to jail.

The second method to benefit from a zone change is not to sit back waiting for one to happen, but to precipitate it. Be bold! Create a vision for what a street, block, or entire suburb may look like if its zoning were changed. Engage architects to come up with conceptual drawings, make models, draw up a plan, invite other property owners to participate, and present it to the city council. People do this all the time, and all of us are benefiting from the previous efforts of other people who have made our towns and cities what they are today.

The most dramatic example of this that I can give is what Property Ventures Limited (PVL), the public company that I founded, is doing near Queenstown, New Zealand. The company took 80 acres of rural land and spent five years getting not just a zoning change but approval from all the local and national governing bodies to build an entire city, complete with supermarkets, movie theatres, a wide range of accommodation options, and everything else that a city needs. The land was originally purchased for NZ$27 million, and the entire project presently has a value of NZ$2.2 billion. Very clearly, the value of the land has, to the benefit of our shareholders, gone through the roof.

Whether you want to capitalize on a minor zone change where you are buying an investment, or apply for and cause a zone change in the style of what PVL is doing in New Zealand, the benefits to you are obvious: You may easily attract a high-paying tenant under a new zone in an area where, under the old zone, a tenant was difficult or even impossible to find.

Split a Single Tenancy into Multiple Tenancies

Sometimes it pays to split large, vacant premises into smaller premises. For instance, depending on market conditions, there may not be much demand for a 10,000-square-foot retail shop. You may in fact have difficulties securing a tenant at, say, $17 psf. However, if you split the space into four units of 2,500 each, it may be easy to find tenants at $24 psf.

Dividing the premises into four units may not be an easy—or cheap—exercise. The dividing walls will need sound- and fire-proofing, each unit will need to be separately metered for electricity and gas, and you will now require four main entrances and four secondary exits for fire egress. However, even if the modifications cost $100,000, it could be well worthwhile. Not only will you have filled the space, generating in this case $240,000 of rental income, but the extra $70,000 of income (over and above what you would have collected had you rented the space to a single tenant at $17 psf), at a cap rate of 8 percent, would increase the value of the building by $875,000.

The funeral parlor discussed earlier is a prime example of splitting a tenancy. Originally, the funeral business had a chapel, offices, a four-bedroom home, a 2,000-square-foot woodworking workshop for the manufacture of coffins, an extra-long garage (to enable a hearse to be loaded out of the rain), and four more over-sized garages. I am sure that previous attempts to secure a tenant had been made on the basis that the tenant would have to lease the entire property. This requirement is no doubt partially why it was so difficult to secure a tenant. I imposed no such obligation. Today, 800 square feet of the workshop building is leased to one tenant with an engraving business, while the remaining 1,200 feet is used as storage. The oversized garages are similarly leased separately. I doubt whether any funeral operator would want to pay the total rent roll—or, for that matter, need the space.

Another example is our own headquarters building in Phoenix. One of my own companies occupied around 2,900 square feet on the ground floor. When we outsourced a large portion of this operation, we moved the remaining staff into a small, 450-square-foot office to maintain a presence in the building. Rather than lease our old space to a single tenant, we split it into two units of around 1,400 square feet and 1,500 square feet. This hardly required any work, as there were already two main entrances and two rear doors. We only had to install a second alarm system, rekey half of the locks, and construct one short partition wall into which we put a door, should one tenant ever in the future want the entire space again. These two suites are occupied by a head-hunting firm and the corporate offices of a very popular cluster of restaurants nearby, at around $24 psf—more than we would likely have achieved with a single tenant occupying the entire space.

Finally, splitting tenancies should not be seen as a way of creating more work for yourself (to set up extra tenants on extra leases) but rather as a way of spreading the investment risk among several tenancies, and increasing the average rental rate.

Consolidate Multiple Tenancies into One

I am not trying to have it both ways, but sometimes you may have difficulties leasing lots of small spaces. In this case, it may be worthwhile consolidating the smaller tenancies into a single, large tenancy.

One of my properties had two retail shops facing a pedestrian-only mall, while the rear of the building faced the street parallel to and behind the mall. A veterinary surgery and pet supply shop occupied the building facing the street, while one of the two retail shops was a music store selling mainly CDs. The music store was not doing particularly well, and the pet shop did not have the benefit of the mall foot-traffic. The solution in this case was to relocate the music store to another property, and to expand the space occupied by the veterinary business into the old music store. Now, pets coming in for grooming or treatment could be driven to the rear entrance, while the portion facing the busy pedestrian mall was ideal for the sale of pets and all the accessories that go with them. (See Figure 7.3.) Each party—music store, pet shop, and landlord—benefitted.

Figure 7.3   **Street Entrances of Veterinary Surgery**

The Ultimate Way to Attract a Tenant

In terms of methods to attract a tenant, I have kept the best until last. This method is so simple and stunningly successful that I occasionally berate myself for not having thought of it sooner.

Remember, with commercial real estate, the value of a property is determined by dividing the rental income by the cap rate. We cannot influence the cap rate—it is determined by the market—but we can do things to improve the rental income. More specifically, if a property is vacant, then its value is very low. Once a tenant is in place paying market rents, then the value of the building can skyrocket.

In other words, it is the rental income—paid by the tenant—that determines the value of a building. The crucial element in this entire operation is the tenant. Without a tenant, you have a building that is almost worthless. In fact, it may be worth less than nothing: If the cost of maintaining the building and paying the property taxes and insurance premiums is greater than the income generated, it is costing you money to own, and it could be argued that you should pay someone to take it off your hands.

Many commercial landlords find themselves in a bind when they have vacant premises for which they can find no tenants. The holding costs can make them go under. If having a building with no tenant is the very worst situation to be in as a commercial investor, then surely the best situation to be in is the exact opposite—having a tenant but no building.

I stumbled upon this concept in the early 1990s, when I had a retail shop for lease. I advertised for a tenant, and soon got a retailer to sign a rental agreement. However, after this tenant had signed up, I kept on receiving calls from more prospective tenants.

At first I dismissed them by saying that the shop was already rented. But then I got thinking—these are all people willing to lease premises from me, and I didn't even ask them exactly what it was they were after.

I told the next person that called that I didn't have anything available, but if he told me in some detail what it was he was after, I could go out and try to find something suitable. And sure enough, within four days I had found a property that I thought would suit him perfectly. He looked at it and agreed, and a month later, he was the happy tenant, and I was the happy landlord, in a building that I acquired for a song as it was vacant at the time of purchase.

In other words, do not focus on acquiring a vacant property, and then try to figure out how to get a tenant for it. Rather, attract the tenant first, and figure out how to get a property for him.

The funeral parlor is an example of the former: I had stumbled across the vacant funeral building, and then set out to find a tenant for it. What I am suggesting here is, find a tenant, determine what he wants, and then find the premises for him. If the property is vacant, you will probably be able to buy the building for next to nothing. With your tenant in place, it should be worth a lot more.

Do not consider this method too bold! If you are open and honest about it, the prospective tenant will be honored that you would go to the effort to find a suitable property for him.

As I write this, I have not one but two of Phoenix's top hairdressers waiting for me to find them suitable premises. Why are they asking me to find them premises, instead of any of hundreds of commercial leasing agents in town? If they go through a commercial leasing agent, they know they will have to pay full market rents on a property. If they go through me, they know that I will find a vacant building that I can buy for a song (because it is vacant), completely renovate it to their specifications and satisfaction, give them a sizable break on market rents, and still make a substantial profit for myself.

Just how do you get people to ask you to find them premises to rent from you? Well, it won't happen by keeping your mouth shut. You have to let people know what you do. This does not mean walking around with a sandwich board stapled to your body, or having your forehead tattooed with "I'll find commercial premises to suit you." Nor do you have to open each conversation with, "Are you by chance looking for commercial premises?" However, it does mean you have to engage the people you come across in conversation. In the case of the hairdressers, the first one told me how much rent was being charged per station, and how little the hairdressers got for the rent they paid. He had a vision of a new kind of salon, which he had shared with his fellow hairdressers, at least half of whom said they would shift to his business if he set it up. I asked him how he hoped to find premises for this operation. He said he was at a loss, and asked if I could offer any suggestions. We are right now looking for the appropriate combination of location, building suitability, and, of course, vacant status of at least part of the building to secure a good purchase price.

The second hairdresser, Bruce Craig, used to be the official hairdresser at Blair House, the official guest quarters of the White House in Washington, D.C. Craig boasts a list of celebrity clients that is astounding, having cut the hair of such well-known people as Hillary Clinton and Mrs. Boris Yeltsin right through to the wife of the former Shah of Iran, former empress Farah Pahlavi. Bruce has ended up in a nondescript salon in the suburbs and is chomping at the bit to have his own salon closer to the heart of all the celebrity action. I recorded one of my weekly video broadcasts from his salon, and he has a great camera presence. Through some contacts, I helped get him a weekly television show in Arizona. Just last week, he had the reigning Miss America on his show, during her last week of holding the title. Clearly, he has sufficient drive and client appeal to ensure that his hairdressing operation will have a high chance of success. Again, I am armed with a great tenant-in-waiting and am on the hunt for a vacant (cheap!) commercial building to put him in.

The more people who know you are in the commercial real estate game, the more will come to you with requests for particular kinds of rental space and offers of vacant properties for sale. I cover this in more detail in Chapter 10, where I talk about how to find deals.

CHAPTER 8

How to Increase Rental Income (and hence the Capital Value)

In Chapter 7 we focused on how you can find a tenant for a vacant property. In this chapter, we consider how you can increase the rental on an existing, tenanted property. Remember, a 10 percent increase in rent equates to a 10 percent increase in capital value (whatever the cap rate!), so any rent increase has a tremendous beneficial effect on your balance sheet.

Naturally, there will be considerable overlap between ideas that can increase the rental on an existing property and those that can attract a tenant in the first place. For instance, the addition of a helipad on the roof of a commercial building may enable rents to be increased on a tenanted building, but if the building was vacant to start off with, it may attract a tenant where otherwise there would be none.

Helipads

Since we have mentioned helipads, let's start with them. To many people, a helipad may seem like an indulgence for the glitterati, but in many parts of the world, helicopter access can be a real business advantage. In Jakarta, Indonesia, for instance, the night-time population of some 10 million swells to about 15 million during the day. The daily influx of 5 million people every morning, and outflow again in the evening, creates traffic jams rivaled only by Bangkok and a few other Asian cities. It can take three hours to cover 10 miles, so that it is often faster to walk. Many do, meaning the footpaths and sidewalks are also jammed full of people. Under these circumstances, a building with a helipad on the roof can command a much higher rent per square meter than a building without such a helipad.

The same is true of New York City, where businessmen on tight time schedules are willing to pay a premium to commute to a local airport by helicopter rather than risk sitting in a traffic jam. Naturally, buildings with a helipad and landing rights command a premium in terms of rent.

The cost of adding a helipad is not so much related to the physical pad itself, but the compliance with regulatory rules such as Federal Aviation Authority or local Civil Aviation Authority requirements. Nonetheless, the return on investment (of both time and money) of getting a helipad added to one of your properties is astounding.

Cell Phone Towers

While we are still on the roofs of buildings, let's talk about cellular telephone towers. Some 20 years ago, a satellite-based phone system called Iridium was devised. It planned to operate 88 low-orbital satellites to relay calls from handheld phones through these satellites to terrestrial base stations so that you could call any land-line or other satellite phone user anywhere on this planet. It sounded like a great idea—and was—but essentially failed because the company never for a moment envisaged that there would be such a tremendous proliferation of terrestrial cellular phone networks. The cell phone, which is also called a mobile phone or handy phone in various parts of the world, has become a part of everyone's lives. It seems that everyone has one! School kids, pilots, valet drivers, you name it. There are more than a billion cell phones in use. Unlike the doomed Iridium, which required only 88 satellites, the worldwide cellular network requires hundreds of thousands of cell phone towers to maintain coverage for the operators' clients. And here is the point: If there are going to be so many cell phone towers, there may as well be some on roofs that you own.

The advantages of having a cellular phone company as a tenant are manifold. First, they pay for and install everything. They cover the cost of any electricity consumed, insurance premiums, lightning protection, and security. Second, they do not occupy any space that you could otherwise rent to tenants. Rather, they mount their antennae on the roof or side of your building. It is money for jam! The rents you will be able to command will be driven by the market and will vary depending on the value of the location. However, $25,000 a year for a suburban location and $150,000 a year for a prominent downtown location are not uncommon rentals. At a cap rate of, say, 10 percent, these rentals would add $250,000 and $1.5 million respectively to the value of your building the day you sign the cellular phone company up as a tenant.

And how exactly do you acquire a cellular phone company as a tenant? I hope you are starting to get the picture that it won't happen by sitting at home with closed doors, watching soaps on television. You may luck out and have a company contact you, but a more proactive approach would be to take some high-quality photos of your rooftop and the commanding views it has over the surrounding area, and then send them (blown up to letter or A4 size, not 6 × 4 inches) along with a letter to every phone company you can think of. At worst they will throw your letter into the trash can. At best they will add $1.5 million to your net worth in the time it takes to record a signature. Television, anyone? (See Figure 8.1.)

Just for the record, I am not so naïve as to suggest that you can safely rent out a cell phone tower and helipad next to each other. The two tend to be mutually exclusive, although many cell phone antennae these days are mounted on the sides of buildings.

More Rooftop Antics

Before leaving the roof, let's brainstorm other items that you can usefully offer for rent up there. News channels want cameras for live monitoring of traffic. Again, approach every television channel in town with photos of the views they would get. Consider

Figure 8.1   Towers with Cellular Antennas and Microwave Dishes

weather stations (to record rainfall, humidity, temperature, wind speed, and volume of air movement). These are leased by newspapers, television stations, or the National Oceanic and Atmospheric Administration. Similarly, you can lease out space for pollution monitoring stations, aeronautical beacons, ham-radio repeater stations, and Wi-Fi antennae to connect branch offices in nearby buildings.

A microwave repeater station to carry telephone bandwidth across town or for a private network can bring in thousands of dollars a month. A satellite dish on the roof may bring in feeds of either video channels or information services to tenants in your building or neighboring buildings.

Once again, you are only limited by your ability to think outside the norm. And instead of finding just one client who wants to rent space on your roof, try to see how many streams of income you can get from each rooftop.

Before we leave the roof, however, there is one more thing you can rent out up there . . .

Naming Rights

An old saying asks, "What's in a name?" but when it comes to commercial real estate, the answer is "a lot of rental income." Whether it be self-centered egotism or smart marketing savvy, many companies are willing to pay ridiculous sums of money to have their name stamped on your building. The Sears Tower, Kodak House, and the Wrigley Building are examples from among millions.

You, as the building owner, can decide whether you should allow the building to have a name and, if so, how much you should try to charge for it. In my experience, while most companies are very meticulous about not paying more than market rental rates for commercial space, they seem to lose all rationality when it comes to wanting the building named after *their* company, and not after the tenants two floors down or three floors up. And, once again, the revenue from the naming rights does not come at the expense of reduced rent elsewhere.

Can you see why I think commercial real estate has so much room for creativity? Every time I see a substantial building without a name, I cringe because I know there is maybe $100,000 per annum waiting to be collected, and the owner is too busy fretting over the latest news bulletin or consumed by writing his own checks to realize that one letter or one phone call could add $1 million of capital value to his property.

Air Space

Just when I thought we were done with the roof and could start to go down into the building, I realized there is more to the roof, namely the space *above* it.

Air space is usually overlooked by property owners because there is nothing there– just thin air. However, when you delve into it, there are many aspects of air space that can generate income.

The most obvious income to be derived from owning air space is simply to sell it, or lease it. Imagine you own a 2-story building that was erected on foundations strong enough to carry a 10-story building. If you didn't have the time, capital, funding capability or inclination to build more stories on the existing 2-story building, then you could simply sell or lease the rights to the space above your existing building. While this may be uncommon in smaller towns and cities, in overcrowded centers such as Manhattan, Montreal, the city of London, Tokyo, and Bangkok, these transactions of air space rights are relatively common.

A less obvious income to be derived from owning air space rights is to sell or lease them, not for the purposes of building in the air space, but specifically to prevent anyone else building anything there.

Imagine a 10-story building in a part of town where the zoning allows for 12 stories—it does not matter whether this building is commercial or residential. Imagine further that every floor of this building except the ground floor (which is used for retail shops) has spectacular views of the adjacent lake (we could be talking about Chicago and Lake Michigan, Geneva and Lake Geneva, or any of hundreds of other cities built beside lakes). Finally, imagine that the only thing between this 10-story tower and the lake is a single-story building that you own. Bearing in mind that zoning allows you to erect a 12-story building on your site, you could lease or sell the air rights to your building to the owners of the neighboring 10-story building. They would be willing to pay a premium for the air rights, simply to prevent their spectacular views of the lake from being blocked. Depending on the relative lot sizes, permitted site-coverage ratios, recession plane restrictions, and a host of other factors, you may well derive more income from leasing the air rights of your building than you would by redeveloping the site and collecting rent. The management overhead would also be about as close to zero as you can get on a commercial transaction.

And, just for the record, air rights are of value for more than just views of a lake. They may be views of mountains, rivers, the ocean, a city, a park, or just wild territory. The point is, where there is a view, people will be willing to pay a premium to ensure they can keep that view.

So far we have covered two instances where air space has commercial value: using the air rights to erect a structure, and using the air rights to prevent the blocking of views *from* a building. A third and far more subtle application of air rights is to prevent the blocking of views *of* a building. Let me illustrate this.

When I was running a three-day commercial real estate course in Sydney, Australia, a couple of years ago, we took all the participants out on buses to look at properties that were on the market then. Looking at real deals makes the process of analyzing a piece of real estate more interesting as it is no longer just theory. The mere possibility that one of the participants (or a consortium) may end up buying the property makes the whole exercise interesting.

One building we looked at was at the top of George Street, close to the Central Railway Station, right next door to the new Mercure Hotel, between Regent Street and Little Regent Street. It was a very narrow, seven-story brick building in mediocre to poor condition, and only 14 percent leased. Normally, this low occupancy rate would excite me, as I would know I could buy the building based on the low occupancy, and soon fill the vacant space to greatly increase the capital value of the building. However, in this case, it was not the low occupancy that excited me, but rather the structure that was placed on the roof.

It was not a helipad, cell phone tower, weather station, traffic cam, microwave repeater station, or any of the other items that we already discussed (and you thought I had covered every conceivable item that could be placed on a roof!). Rather, this structure was a huge billboard. Now, at an elevation of seven stories above the road, this billboard could be seen for miles, especially by travelers in the tens of thousands of cars and buses who commuted into downtown Sydney every day along the very busy Broadway. This billboard is in one of the prime locations in Sydney for an advertising hoarding. Furthermore, city by-laws in Sydney ensure that existing billboards are grandfathered in, but new billboards are extremely difficult to get approval on, making existing billboards even more valuable. The rental on the billboard alone was A$523,000 per annum. Based on a modest cap rate of 10 percent, the rent from this billboard would add more than A$5 million to the value of the building.

Everyone in the course got excited. Some participants started canvassing the others to see if there was any interest in forming a syndicate to buy the property. The event promoters got wind of this and made inquiries as to the potential legal consequences of such a syndicate purchase being made at an educational event. They no doubt did this because the Australian Securities and Investment Commission was clamping down hard on investments being offered at seminars, in the wake of some spectacular collapses of investment vehicles that had been offered at other promoters' events.

While all this energy was being dissipated, I was concerned with something else. The Mercure Hotel already blocked any view of the billboard from the northeast. On the west side of the seven-story building was a two-story art-deco building. What if this building was demolished and replaced with an eight- or ten-story structure? It would obliterate any views of the billboard from the west, kill the rental income stream generated by the building, and thus knock the A$5 million off the value of the property.

It appeared that just over A$80,000 per annum was being paid to the building owners next door for their air rights. Which brings me to my point: Air rights can be valuable not just to build on, or to prevent views *from* your property being blocked, but also to prevent views *of* your building (and in this case billboard) being blocked.

Once again, don't just sit around waiting for neighboring owners to offer you fees for your air rights. As the owner of the building with the billboard in Sydney, would you not be willing to give up $80,000 of your rental income from the billboard, in order to maintain the remaining A$443,000?

That may not be the end of the transactions regarding the billboard, though. The A$80,000 that the neighbor receives for air rights may well be more than his other income from that property. At a 10 percent cap rate, the income stream might therefore be worth A$800,000 to him. He may also realize that if, for whatever reason, you tore down the billboard, he would lose his $80,000 per annum air rights income, and thus A$800,000 of his capital value. Consequently, he may be willing to sell you his old building at an advantageous price—more than anyone else would likely be willing to pay (since buying this building will save you $80,000 a year, a benefit not enjoyed by any other purchaser), but less than his total income including air rights divided by market cap rates (since he realizes that any other purchaser would not see the $80,000 as a guaranteed income stream).

Parking

Frequently with office space, the rental dollars per square foot figure is partially determined by the number of car parks available (per thousand square feet or some other area measure). This is particularly true in cities with a dense downtown, such as Los Angeles, Chicago, Atlanta, or New York City. Find out what these ratios are for your buildings, and then see if it is appropriate to provide more car parks. One option would be to sacrifice one or several lower floors of a multistory office building and turn them into car parks. The increased rent per square foot on the remaining floors may more than compensate the lost rental income from the erstwhile offices.

Or there may be a vacant building next door to your property, of a standard insufficient to use for commercial office purposes. However, the building may easily be converted into a parking building with walkway access to your office tower. In the 1990s, I was involved with an offer to acquire the Bank One tower in downtown Fort Worth, Texas. This beautiful, octagonal-shaped 37-story building with views for miles around had an anomaly—it boasted relatively few car parks, severely limiting the rent per square foot, and therefore the capital value, of the entire building. Nearby, however, was a semiderelict building that everyone thought was an eyesore, and no one could figure out what to do with it.

I am assuming I do not need to detail what use we had for this nearby building! By the way, are you getting a sense of how commercial real estate has lots of room for thinking outside the box, and for creating something out of nothing, even though it was under everyone's nose all the time?

We missed out on the Bank One tower, and were shocked to see a short time later that a tornado had passed through town and blown out nearly every window in that beautiful tower. For a while it was slated for demolition, which would have made it the tallest building in the United States to be demolished, but it was ultimately spared that fate and was converted into residential units.

Japan has a population about 40 percent of that of the United

States, crammed onto a land mass about the size of California, with only 16 percent of the land being habitable. This results in chronic shortages of space, tiny homes, tiny offices, and, of course, major parking problems.

The Japanese, being ingenious at just about anything they do, have come up with some brilliant solutions. The first time I saw what is a standard facility in Japan, my mind went spinning as to where else we could apply this technology.

While parking buildings in the West are mainly of the self-park variety, requiring lots of wasted space for two lanes of traffic around the parks and generous ramps to drive between floors, in Japan most parks are automated. One variety that can be installed against the blank wall of a high-rise building is just over one car-length deep, and two and a half car-widths wide, yet it can safely store 20, 50, or even more cars (depending on the height of the building). The system consists of an elevator with multiple cages in a continuous loop (like the Paternoster elevators popular in Europe in the first half of the twentieth century[1]) where you drive your car onto a platform, and then your car (and all the others) is moved around, a bit like on a Ferris wheel, except in a vertical loop rather than a circular loop. When your car is placed in the elevator, you receive a card coded to your platform; when you return, you insert the card in a slot, and your car gets moved around on this elevator system until it is once more at the bottom. The car is backed out, spun around on a circular platform, and you are ready to get on your way. (See Figure 8.2.)

Not only is this a very efficient way of parking cars (imagine how much area would be needed to park 50 cars in a conventional

---

[1]Many Paternoster elevators are still in use in Europe—photos and web references are given at www.dolfderoos.com.

Figure 8.2   **Entrance to Japanese Car-Parking System (Note the rotating platform to spin your car around when you back out).**

parking building), but there are many other advantages as well from both a user and operator point of view.

First, theft of vehicles or contents is no longer a problem (not that it was a problem in Japan in the first place, but elsewhere!), as no one gets to climb up into the parking structure. Second, all the unsavory activities often associated with parking buildings—muggings, assaults, and drug deals, to name a few—are eliminated. Third, no one runs out of gas in the elevator system (car engines are turned off) or locks their keys in the car (keys can be left inside the unlocked vehicle or given to an attendant). Fourth, your car is not subject to being dented by the careless driving of other users of the parking system. Similarly, your panels will not be dented by the opening of doors of adjacent cars, trucks, and beat-up old bombs, be it a genuine accident, a more nonchalant "I don't care about other people's cars," or a more spiteful "Why does he get to drive a car like that? I'll show him."

To be sure, the Japanese-style car-parking buildings cost a lot more than a sealed parking lot at ground level, which explains why, in cities where land has traditionally been very cheap, like Phoenix, there are many parking lots, and, to my knowledge, not a single automated parking machine. However, the Japanese system of parking is finding more and more application in other parts of the world, partially as cities get more cramped for space, and partially as people find out that they exist and discover their benefits.

A parking system like this for some 50 cars costs around $500,000—not cheap, by any standard. However, let's work some numbers. Imagine you have a 12,000-square-foot office building and there are only four parking spaces per 1,000 square feet. This is considered a low ratio of car parks in many parts of the world. Imagine that with this low ratio, rents are limited to $12 per square foot. Imagine further that if you could increase the ratio to eight parking spaces per 1,000 square feet, the rent would climb to $18 per square foot. The car park would therefore increase the rental income from $144,000 per annum to $216,000 per annum in terms of base rental. Depending on the location, you may also be able to charge for each parking space. At a modest $50 per month, the additional 48 parking spaces would bring in an extra $28,800 per annum. Combined with the increase in base rent of $72,000, we are talking about an extra $100,800 a year, and suddenly the $500,000 capital outlay seems to be not too bad. There will be some maintenance issues, to be sure, but then again you can capitalize and depreciate the structure, resulting in taxation benefits.

Another parking structure that I have come across in Singapore also involves elevators. The elevator cabin has both a front door and a rear door. At ground level, you drive your car into the cabin of the elevator, and it then spirits you up to a flat roof perhaps six stories high. The other door of the cabin then opens, and you can drive forward and straight out onto the roof of the building to park your car. This utilizes the space on the roof that would otherwise go unused, and does not require a ramp to spiral up six floors to get to the roof. Photos of this system can be found on our web site, www.dolfderoos.com.

Of course, not all elevator systems need be this expensive or elaborate. A more common system in the United States in congested cities like New York is for a hydraulic (or mechanical) lifter to elevate one car up in the air, so that another can park underneath. (See Figure 8.3.) The obvious downside is that for the elevated car to be able to leave, the one beneath it has to be moved. However, the fact that these parking systems exist and are in use is a testament to their cost effectiveness for their owners. I have seen, in New York, cars stacked four high using this system.

New York, while an obvious place for stacked parking systems, is not the only part of the country where they can be found. In Florida, for instance, with an increasing shortage of space spurred in part by ongoing immigration (both domestic and international from all parts of the world, especially South America), the concept is gaining popularity. (See Figure 8.4.)

All this talk of stacking cars vertically should not stifle lateral thinking. It is not just cars that can be stacked in a vertical parking system—boats are also contenders for this technology, as the accompanying photo shows. (See Figure 8.5.)

Figure 8.3   Four-Layer Stacked Parking System, New York City

Figure 8.4   Dual-Layer Stacked Car-Parking System, Miami, Florida

Figure 8.5   **Quad-Layer Stacked Boat-Parking System**

In fact, when the value of real estate goes high enough, more things than just vehicles get stacked vertically. Apartments and condominiums are an obvious example of having many units share the same piece of dirt, as are car parks and boat parks. However, the concept permeates through other areas of life, and even the afterlife. In St. Tropez, for instance, land is so expensive that many tombs are stacked on top of each other. (See Figure 8.6.)

While even thinking of someone's resting place in this light may seem somewhat invasive, bear in mind that in most parts of the world, cemeteries are privately owned, and are therefore just

Figure 8.6   **Triple-Layer Stacked Tombs, St. Tropez, France**

as much commercial real estate operations as a retail store or office complex.

The Humble Webcam

A webcam is simply a camera, but instead of recording images onto film, or onto memory the way digital cameras do, they transmit images over the Internet. Cheap webcams can be acquired for $50 or less and may require a computer to transmit their images. You can also spend hundreds of dollars on webcams that have superlative optics, tremendous zoom capabilities, and remote pan, tilt, and zoom control, and that do not require a computer to transmit images—they are connected directly to the Internet and feed their images to anyone who has user-name and password access.

Webcams have, of course, been put to many creative money-making uses. There are also many great applications for increasing the rent on commercial properties.

Perth in Western Australia is a surprisingly modern and bustling city, with a burgeoning economy that is largely driven by the enormous and lucrative mining industry that extracts uranium, nickel, cobalt, gold, and many other minerals out of the ground. Perth's international passenger airport is busy enough, with direct flights from many parts of Australia, Asia, and Europe, but there is another airport at Perth called Jandakot, which mainly operates as a base for service organizations such as the Royal Flying Doctor Service, Department of Environment and Conservation Forest and Bushfire Patrol, and the Western Australia Police Air Support unit. Jandakot is also an important training base for international airline pilots, with Singapore Airlines and China Southern Airlines operating flying colleges and student accommodation facilities at the airport. Last year, the airport recorded over 400,000 aircraft movements, making it the busiest airport in Australia.

For many years I was on the lecture circuit in Australia, and during my visits to Perth I became acquainted with Jim Poignand and Katie Moustakas through some business dealings. We ended up joining forces on numerous projects, including Australia's number one investment property web site, www.Landlord Central.com.au. One of our projects is the building of aircraft hangars at Jandakot Airport. (See Figures 8.7 through 8.9.)

Figure 8.7   Hangars Being Constructed at Jandakot Airport near Perth

Figure 8.8   Completed Hangar with Aircraft Inside

Figure 8.9   **Another View of the Hangars**

Now a hangar is a hangar anywhere in the world—it usually consists of a concrete slab, walls with some kind of metal skin, and a huge sliding door on the side offering access to the runway. In general, the rent you can expect from a hangar is dictated by the market forces of supply and demand. However, I kept thinking that there had to be a way to increase the rental income from a hangar.

Based on the land value and construction cost of a hangar, the rent should not be that high. However, tenants tend not to store old files or secondhand furniture in hangars, but rather airplanes—sometimes expensive multimillion-dollar jet airplanes. If you stored your $20 million Gulfstream G4 jet in a hangar, would you not want to know that it was safe? Enter the webcam!

A webcam installed in a hangar gives those with password access the ability to see what is going on inside the hangar. It can be accessed from anywhere in the world, day or night. What is more, it can be programmed such that whenever movement is detected, a photo is taken and e-mailed to any number of e-mail addresses. This gives the owner of the $20 million plane the peace of mind that any activity will be recorded. Furthermore, by mounting a thermometer and hydrometer near the web cam, a user can pan the camera to see what the readings are, to satisfy themselves that their baby is not being roasted or frozen.

If you owned an expensive airplane, what would it be worth to you to have webcam access to your hangar? We have found no resistance to an extra $500 per month, which is a good return on a $600 webcam and a $50 per month broadband access fee.

I have also installed webcams in storage facilities, office complexes, car parking facilities, and retail shops, in each case receiving a return on investment that is astounding.

Interior Remodel

There are many things you can do to increase the value of a commercial property to prospective tenants. When we bought a commercial building in Phoenix for our own headquarters, there were a number of tenancies already in place, including a law firm, an architect, and a real estate developer. (See Figure 8.10.) However, there were also two suites totaling 2,400 square feet whose interiors had been totally demolished, with pipes and cables dangling everywhere, some still connected, and some obviously having been disused for years.

The fact that these suites were not just vacant but looked like a demolition site and were therefore not able to be rented no doubt contributed to us being able to acquire the property for a song at

Figure 8.10　**Office Building in Phoenix Where We Remodeled Suites**

$1.25 million. We then set about remodeling these suites. (See Figure 8.11.)

With all the two-by-four studs exposed (the dry wall panels had been stripped out), it was a perfect time to rewire for electricity, telephone, and internet. This is where some owners skimp. Many landlords think, for instance, that one Ethernet outlet in each room should be sufficient. Well, it may be for a tanning clinic or a storeroom, but for many firms these days, one outlet won't cut it. These days, each worker in an office tends to have his own com-

Figure 8.11   **Interior of Suite (Note soundproofed air-conditioning ducts.)**

puter connected to the Internet. Apart from computers, we are now connecting to the office network by way of voice over Internet protocol (VoIP) phones, Internet cameras, shared printers, copiers, fax machines, and remote terminals. We even have some of the air-conditioning control units in our buildings connected to the Internet so that we can monitor and control them remotely. All of these devices require an Internet connection, so one Ethernet outlet per room is hopelessly inadequate.

We place one Ethernet outlet (an RJ-45 socket) every yard or meter along the walls. This may seem like overkill, but the marginal cost in terms of extra cable, RJ-45 sockets, and contractor time to install everything is next to nothing. We bring all the cables together at a patch panel, where the tenants can connect any Ethernet outlet of their choosing to their network.

Furthermore, neither of the two demolished suites had kitchen facilities. Having running water and a sink within a tenant's premises is not necessary to attract a tenant, but it may just appeal to some prospective tenants and tip the balance in terms of their decision to rent from you. I, for one, would much rather have my own kitchen facilities in an office than shared facilities with a host of other tenants, let alone no facilities at all.

So, in both suites, we added a full kitchen with sink, hot and cold water, cupboards, refrigerator, and dishwasher. (See Figure 8.12.) In case you think a dishwasher is an extravagance, we bought these brand-new at $170 each. We all know what it is like to want a drink, and to see all of the office's 13 cups unwashed in the sink because no one has taken the effort to clean up after use. A dishwasher circumvents these issues, and is probably more hygienic than washing by hand, anyway.

We also put in new ducting for the air-conditioning. The ceilings were too low to hide them above false panels, so the ductwork was exposed. Ducting can be relatively noisy, so we set out to find soundproofed ducting. Surprisingly, to install ducting with a solid inch of rubberized sound proofing material lining the entire insides only cost $960 extra for the entire two suites. You can barely hear when the air-conditioning plant is on.

With the drywall gone, we decided to upgrade the fire wall separating the two suites, and to put an internal doorway between the suites, just in case a single tenant ever ended up leasing both suites—this way they would have internal access instead of having to go through both front doors to get from one to the other. Again, we did not skimp. We put in dual solid doors with a six-

Figure 8.12   **Kitchen Including Dishwasher Added to Office Suite**

inch space between them, with rubber seals for both soundproofing and fireproofing.

Finally, we weather-sealed all exterior doors, installed recessed lighting, put in high-security locks, and had an interior decorator advise on the color of the carpet and the two-tone walls.

The total cost of this remodel and fit-out for the two suites came to just under $68,000. We placed a "For Lease" sign on the lawn in front of the building, and before long a lady who operates a high-end children's store down the road stopped by our office in the same building and inquired about the suite we had for lease, on behalf of her husband, who runs a high-tech company. A combination of the location, style of the building, fit-out, and technology features must have swayed them, as they signed up straight away on a three-year lease for the larger of the two suites.

The other suite was already leased. However, when this lease came up for renewal, the tenants decided not to renew, and the technology firm next door snapped up the space. I have no idea whether the internal access between the suites and our catering to high-tech features swayed them or not, and at the end of the day it doesn't really matter. The suites generate around $20 per square foot, which over an area of 2,400 square feet equates to an income of $48,000 per annum—not bad for an outlay of $68,000. Not only are the returns good, but the extra $48,000 of income, based on market cap rates of around 8 percent, has increased the value of the building by $600,000.

Adding features and facilities to buildings can increase the likelihood of attracting a tenant in the first place, and also of getting a better rental per square foot. I feel so strongly about this, and believe there are so many ways of achieving this, that I have written an entire book on this subject (*101 Ways to Massively Increase the Value of Your Real Estate without Spending Much Money*, Time Life Direct, 2002). Every time you can get more rent, not only does your cash flow increase, but so does the capital value of your building.

In New Zealand, we have one building completely fitted out with electronic locks. They use what is known as a *scramble keypad*, where the digits 1 through 9 plus zero are presented in random positions each time the electronic lock is accessed, so that anyone looking on cannot determine which digits you pressed from the pattern of hand movements you make while entering your code. This system has a number of benefits. No longer do we have the problem of tenants (or their staff) losing keys and therefore compromising the security of the building or requiring the locks to be rekeyed. Each user can have a different code, and when he leaves the company (voluntarily or otherwise) his code is simply made inactive and he can no longer gain access. Furthermore, each code can be set up to be active only at certain times, so that the janitors, for instance, who come between 5 P.M. and 7 P.M., will not be able to gain access at midnight. We can also run a log to see who came on any given day, and at which time. Finally, we can access the control system through the Internet, so that if we need to give access to, say, an electrician after hours, we can set up a code that will work for him without having to meet him at the building to give him access.

Whether tenants will pay you more rent if you install electronic locks depends a lot on both the location of the building and the likely category of tenant that building will attract. It is a matter of finding out what tenants want, and then catering to that if the numbers work in your favor.

One of the first projects that my public company, Property Ventures Limited, undertook when we started nearly a decade ago was to convert a derelict factory into upscale student accommodation. To know which direction to head in, Dave Henderson, the creative and energetic impetus heading the company, organized focus group meetings, where the company met with students to find out what it was that they wanted in accommodation. Some of their feedback was enlightening. For instance, most student dorms have single beds, and everyone knows that a lot of dorm walls get damaged as students replace these with double beds. Regardless of any moral implications you may think of, you can save a lot of damage to your building, and enjoy a lower vacancy rate and higher rental income, if you simply put in the kind of bed that most hotels and motels have by default.

Similarly, the students relished unlimited and free nationwide phone calls, unlimited high-speed Internet access, and high security on the building itself. Interestingly enough, the cost of providing these features was minimal. And yet, from the day we opened the doors on this first facility, occupancy rates have been the highest in the industry, and we have opened three more, including a custom-built $15.4 million building that has set new standards for student accommodation.

After a while, deciding what features to add to a property to increase its rental income and therefore its capital value is not so much a matter of going through a checklist as it is a way of thinking. All it takes is a bit of creativity, and creativity is a lot like a muscle—the more you use it, the stronger it becomes. By all means, go through a checklist, but also try to come up with one new idea or concept for each building.

The Triple Win of Alarm Systems

Alarms systems are a very interesting example of something you can do to a building at zero cost to yourself, while increasing the value of your premises to your tenants and to yourself.

Most business alarms are monitored, meaning an alarm condition is transmitted to a central monitoring station, where the condition giving rise to the alarm is evaluated and appropriate action taken. This is much safer than an alarm that merely has audible and visual signals at the premises indicating a break-in or fire, because after hours there may not be many people around to notice the alarm condition in the first place, and even if there are, it is often assumed to be a false alarm.

Most alarm companies will install an alarm free of charge if you are willing to sign up for a contract to have the alarm monitored by that company. Furthermore, most prospective commercial tenants prefer to have their premises alarmed and monitored to safeguard their staff, files, computers, and stock.

Consequently, when you get an alarm installed free of charge to you, and have the tenant pay the monthly monitoring fee, then everyone wins. The alarm company wins, as they get another client. The tenants win, as they are happy to pay more in rent for premises with an alarm, even if they pay the monthly monitoring fee. And you as landlord win, as you are collecting more rent, have a building that is less likely to be broken into, and have a tenant who is less likely to leave.

It should come as no surprise that most of my commercial premises are fitted with alarm systems.

Rent Reviews to Market

Usually, when you acquire a commercial property, it is tempting to assume the rentals were brought up to market levels at the time of the last rent review. But this is not necessarily the case.

As part of your due diligence in deciding whether to buy a property, you should compare existing rents at the property with market rentals (more on this in Chapter 11). If rents on your newly acquired property are below market levels, then by all means bring them up to market at the next rent review. This can be the fastest and simplest method of increasing the rental income from your property—after all, it only requires a couple of signatures on a rent review document, and an alteration to the amount automatically transferred to your bank account each month.

Occasionally we come across buildings where the rents are 40 percent or more below market levels. This may have come about because the owners were simply unaware of market rentals, or they have become familiar with the tenants and don't want to offend them, or they are absentee owners and they have simply forgotten about rent reviews, or the management has been left to a young relative who is more interested in partying than in undertaking boring rent reviews. Whatever the reason, relish the fact that this happens, because it has probably contributed to your managing to acquire the building for less than its true market value.

Obviously, when you bring these rents up to market levels, you are going to meet a lot of resistance from tenants, and even accusations of being unfair. They will say things like, "We haven't had a rent increase in years, and now you are trying to hit us with a 30 percent rent increase when inflation is only 3 percent. That is blatantly unfair! Just who do you think you are?"

Your response should simply be that you are not burdening them with an unfair and unjustified 30 percent rental increase. Rather, they have enjoyed a somewhat unfair (to the landlord) 30 percent rental discount to market levels. I have never lost a tenant as a result of sometimes substantial increases of rent to market levels, for the simple reason that the tenants either know or soon find out that if they were to seek other premises, they would have to pay market rental rates there as well. They realize they were onto a great thing, and are just reluctant to give it up.

We could go on for page after page of examples of what you can do to increase the value of your buildings, but I think I have made it clear enough: Anytime you can increase the rental on a property, you increase the capital value. Next, it is time to start to bring the opening chapters together.

CHAPTER 9

What Were the Disadvantages of Commercial Real Estate?

You will recall from Chapter 3 that there are many tremendous benefits of investing in commercial real estate as opposed to residential real estate. In Chapter 4, we saw that there were two perceived disadvantages: It can be difficult to attract a tenant to a commercial property, and banks tend to offer a much lower loan-to-value (LTV) ratio on commercial real estate, meaning that you have to put up a higher proportion of the purchase price in cash. Here are my responses to those perceived disadvantages.

The fact that people find it difficult to attract tenants to commercial real estate works in your favor. Existing owners of vacant buildings, their leasing agents, real estate agents trying to sell the building, and other prospective buyers have shown through their actions (or inaction) that they cannot find a tenant. They all believe with a passion that finding a tenant is difficult, and consequently, the property can be bought for much less than if it were tenanted.

What more could you ask for? All of these people (and, to put it bluntly, their ignorance on how to attract a tenant) work in your favor. You, however, know how to attract a tenant, or at the very least know what steps you can take to dramatically increase the chances of getting a tenant. In many instances, you do not even have to go unconditional on the purchase of a property until you have secured a tenant. In other words, you can buy a property that is on the market for $1 million, knowing full well that once your tenant (whom you have already lined up and maybe even signed up on some legal document) is in place, the property will be worth $2 million.

To put it yet another way, you can buy an asset for $1 million that is truly worth $1 million to a seller, knowing that to you it is worth $2 million. That sounds like a great deal to me. In other words, the perception that it is difficult to find a tenant enables you to acquire commercial real estate at incredibly low prices.

So what about the second perceived disadvantage, namely that banks will only lend maybe 60 percent on a commercial building?

When it comes to residential real estate, banks lend on *the lesser of* the appraised value or the purchase price. Their reasoning is that if you buy a property for $400,000, then that is exactly what the market has determined that property to be worth. If you claim it is in fact worth $550,000, the bank will disagree, pointing out that no one else was willing to pay more than $400,000 for it, so the market has proven that it is worth only that much. Even if you get an appraisal from a registered appraiser, the bank will respond that appraisers can get it wrong or even be induced to suggest a higher value, and will reiterate that the market has shown this property to be worth only $400,000.

What is more, if this residential property was vacant when you bought it, you cannot claim that you got it for a song because it was vacant, and that as soon as you get a tenant in it, it will be worth $550,000. That argument won't fly for the simple reason, as we have seen, that a vacant house is worth about as much as that same house tenanted.

Consequently, banks will look at the lower of the appraised value and the purchase price in determining the value for mortgage purposes. Now, admittedly, they are happy to lend 80 percent of this lower value without requiring mortgage insurance, and, if you are willing to pay mortgage insurance, will lend a lot more than 80 percent—even 100 percent and higher.

Compared with residential real estate, it does seem on the surface as though buying commercial real estate should be more difficult, as banks typically lend only 60 percent of the value. However, imagine you buy a vacant commercial property for $1 million, and you secure a tenant willing to pay $200,000 per annum. If market cap rates are 10 percent, then an appraisal will show the building to be worth $2 million. Under these circumstances, 9 out of 10 banks will agree that the true value is now $2 million. The rationale goes along the lines that without a tenant, the building truly was worth only $1 million, being made up of residual land value, building value, and *potential* to find a tenant. However, with a cap rate of 10 percent and an annual income of $200,000, the property truly is worth $2 million. In this case, banks sensibly accept that even though you paid a lot less for it, the purchase price is largely irrelevant in determining the present, fully tenanted value.

Who cares if banks only lend 60 percent of the valuation for mortgage purposes, if they accept that your building is worth $2 million even though you only paid $1 million? They are willing to lend you $1.2 million on an asset that has only cost you $1 million. You would in fact be able to pocket $200,000, tax free and legally.

This is why I refer to these two so-called disadvantages as *perceived disadvantages*. In fact, they work in your favor. It just depends on how you look at it.

So, to our list in Chapter 3 of advantages of commercial real estate over residential real estate, we can now add two more:

1. Sellers of commercial real estate, their leasing agents, real estate agents, and other investors looking to buy commercial real estate all have this notion that it is difficult to find tenants for commercial space, and therefore they downgrade the value of anything you are looking at buying that is vacant. Consequently, vacant commercial real estate can be bought for a fraction of what it is worth to you fully tenanted.

2. Banks are willing to lend you more than you pay for a commercial property, so long as the valuation for mortgage purposes is based on actual rental income divided by market cap rates. They are not concerned with what you paid for it, but rather what the rental income is and what cap rates are.

Whew! I almost feel as though it has taken me up to here in this book to point out all the advantages of commercial real estate, and to counter the two perceived disadvantages that everyone I come across spouts out.

Now that we agree that commercial real estate is the way to go, let's look at a few aspects of finding, analyzing, negotiating, funding, and managing commercial real estate.

CHAPTER 10

Finding Commercial Real Estate

The most frequent question I get asked when people hear I have found another great commercial deal is, "How did you find it?" The truth is there is no one best method for finding great deals. I advocate using a combination of different methods.

Newspaper Advertisements

It pays to keep your eye on the newspaper to see what kinds of properties are being offered for sale. I found my smallest commercial real estate deal this way.

I came across a small column advertisement in a Saturday newspaper for a "wet fish supply shop" (where they only sell raw fish). The advertisement simply read, "Commercial investment, $59,000, 17 percent return, phone xxx-xxxx, ABC Realty." I found this advertisement at about 8 P.M. that Sunday night and called straight away. My opening line was, "I suppose the property is gone by now."

To my surprise, the answer was, "No, sir, you are the first person to have bothered to call." We decided it was too late that night to look at it, but arranged to meet at 8 A.M. the next day.

There was nothing wrong with the building. While the total area was only 800 square feet (for both the land and buildings), the tenant had been there for years, a standard commercial lease was

Figure 10.1   **Wet Fish Supply Shop**

in place, and the property was on a busy corner with about 20,000 cars going by every day. (See Figures 10.1 and 10.2.) The owner, I was told, was selling owing to health issues. While I normally might make an offer on a property below the asking price, in this case, in deference to the seller's health, and because it was such a good deal in the first place, I signed a contract to buy it at the full $59,000.

The lease was a triple-net lease, and the rental income of $10,400 per annum was therefore net. I showed the lease to a bank, and they capped the income out at 13 percent, giving the building

Figure 10.2   **Close-Up of the Fish Shop**

a valuation of $80,000 ($10,400 divided by 13 percent). They offered me a 70 percent mortgage, giving me $56,000. Now remember I only paid $59,000 for the property, so the bank was willing to fund all but the last $3,000.

While my return on investment by definition was 17.63 percent ($10,400 of income divided by a purchase price of $59,000), after paying the mortgage, I was left with around $5,000 per annum, so my cash-on-cash return was actually $5,000 of net income divided by a capital outlay of only $3,000, or a whopping 167 percent. That is a good return by anyone's reckoning.

I still own the building, as I have a theory that people who sell real estate tend to live to regret it. Taking the time to read the small column advertisements that day certainly paid off with this building.

Note that often the properties advertised in small columns will be far more lucrative than those advertised in big display ads. This is probably because the chance of finding a bargain is much smaller once a battery of experts have debated and discussed what the asking price should be and how large the advertisement should be. Column advertisements tend to be placed by individuals who are looking at saving the expense of a large marketing campaign. On the surface they are right—a tiny advertisement does cost a lot less than a half-page display ad, and by selling it without the help of a real estate agent or firm, they will save themselves a commission. However, they also risk getting a much lower price for their property, as large display advertisements and the power and resources of a good real estate firm can usually attract a larger pool of potential buyers, better negotiation skills, and a better understanding of market values to begin with.

Another property I sourced through a small advertisement in the "Investments for Sale" column simply stated, "Commercial investment, $12,000, 16 percent return net, 5 year lease, phone xxx-xxxx." The price, of course, seemed ridiculously low, and I almost didn't bother to call. However, I have a policy of calling on all ads that have potential, because even if 19 out of 20 do turn out to be misprints, decoys, or lures to solicit phone calls from investors who may turn out to be good leads, about 1 in 20 turns out to be an excellent investment. So I phoned the number and got hold of the agent, who immediately confessed that the $12,000 was a misprint and should have read $120,000. However, he assured me, the returns were genuinely 16 percent.

I arranged to meet the agent on-site the next afternoon, a Sunday, and after waiting for half an hour past the appointed time and getting no response from his phone, gave up and went home. When I called him the next day, he apologized and stated that he had simply forgotten about the appointment. Now if you are prone to getting irritated easily, having the attitude, "I'll show this good-for-nothing agent who is the boss! Forget it, I don't care how good the deal is, I am not working with him!" then you could miss out on some great deals. My attitude is more along the lines of, "Great! With incorrect advertisements and a sloppy attitude about turning up at appointments, my competition will be decimated!" In the case of this particular building, the agent even revealed that he had no one else interested in the property (thanks to his single insertion of an advertisement with a misprint in the small column of a local newspaper, and his forgetfulness toward appointments). This knowledge gave me even more bargaining power, and I ended up owning the property with a 22 percent return on investment, as detailed in Chapter 12 on negotiations.

Real Estate Firms

Another good source of leads is to be on the mailing lists of both large and small commercial real estate brokerages to see what they have on their books. Also, look in the commercial section of realty magazines, and stay in regular contact with the handful of agents who will understand what it is you are looking for.

I am baffled by the number of people who claim to shy away from using real estate agents on the grounds that they do not like paying commissions. For heaven's sake, the seller pays the commission,[1] so lose the attitude!

Another common question I get is how to choose a real estate agent. Again, there is no hard and fast rule. The best thing to do is to interview them. By this I do not mean sitting them down for a formal interview, but rather meeting with them, having a chat, and getting a feel for whether the two of you will be a good match.

For instance, a lot of investors refuse to deal with a real estate agent who is himself an investor, on the grounds that should the agent come across a listing that is a real bargain, he will snap it up himself rather than pass it on to you. While I am sure there must be instances where this has happened, the risk of losing a bargain to your agent will be overwhelmingly compensated by the commensurate advantages of dealing with an agent who understands what investing is all about.

An investor-agent will not waste your time with inane com-

---

[1]There are some exceptions, such as Belgium, where both the buyer and the seller pay a commission, but in most countries, the commission is paid by the seller.

ments like, "It must be a good deal as otherwise the seller would be asking more." An investor-agent understands your need for cash flow and will even offer leads on potential tenants, knowing that if you can marry the tenant to the property he is trying to sell you, he will get one or maybe two commissions (the selling commission and the leasing commission).

An investor-agent may come to you with a property that he would dearly like to acquire, but he simply does not have the resources on his own to do so. A lucrative partnership may result, where his firm even offers to do the management at "mates rates" (a discounted fee).

So during your informal interview with prospective agents, get a feel for whether the agent is truly excited about the potential of real estate and will therefore go the extra mile to ferret out a great deal, source a tenant, or figure out a twist on a property that may change its use or otherwise increase its value, or whether being a real estate agent is just a job for him that pays the bills. Your success in real estate will depend partially on your skills at choosing an agent who understands what it is you do.

Whenever I am in a new city or region, I will often step into a real estate firm's office (chosen at random) and simply ask the receptionist who would be the best commercial investment agent there. If she hesitates, let alone states that they don't deal in investment real estate, I simply move on. Usually, though, she will choose someone and introduce me.

I then proceed to ask this agent, "What would be the top three investment properties you have on your books right now?" If he leans back in his chair, puts his hands behind his head, kicks his feet onto his desk (revealing white shoes), and says with a smirk, "They are all good investment properties—now how much do you have to spend today?" then once again, I move on.

However, if he thinks it over and states, "It would have to be these three. Take this one, for instance," showing me photos and a file of the property he is talking about, "it has been on the market for over three months. Similar buildings in the vicinity are selling for $2.6 million, and yet this one can't muster much interest at $2.1 million. And yet it has better freeway access, a new air-conditioning plant, and a high security fence around the perimeter." Now this agent seems to understand what constitutes a great investment.

Finding great agents is a matter of trial and error. Also, as time goes on, people evolve, and great agents may lose interest in the game (or may have made so much money they can opt out) while previously mediocre agents may become experts and useful allies. Always keep an open mind, but at the same time ensure you are dealing with agents who can support your goal of increasing your equity, collateral, and cash flow through the judicious acquisition of commercial real estate.

The Internet

The more you can catch yourself saying, "I remember a time when . . . ," the more you realize you are getting inexorably older. When I got started in real estate, there was no Internet, and not even any cell phones. While there were many advantages to that relatively primitive age, we are not here to debate the relative merits. The reality is that we do have cell phones and the Internet, and if you want to be competitive, you have to embrace these new technologies or be overtaken by those who can find and transact deals faster than you ever dreamt possible with your mentality stuck in the past.

The Internet is in fact a great resource when it comes to real estate. It is entirely possible to search listings online, evaluate deals, submit offers, conduct due diligence, apply for finance, arrange insurance, attract tenants, and manage the property, all completely over the Internet. Furthermore, since it no longer matters whether you are in the next building, down the road, across town, or halfway around the world, the Internet has made it possible to invest in other countries without needing to have a physical presence there. This latter phenomenon—the ease of investing abroad largely because of the Internet—has created great opportunities for investors. We explore foreign real estate investments in Chapter 22.

Keep your eye on the Internet and the many sites that offer commercial real estate for sale. As time goes on, the Internet is becoming increasingly popular as a means of sifting through listings. This means that more and more properties offered for sale will be able to be found on the Internet. Unfortunately, the commensurate disadvantage is that it is now also a lot easier for everyone else to find these listings. Having said that, it is still worthwhile studying these properties, as it gives you a feel for where the market is at, and every now and then you will still find a bargain that meets your criteria.

Just as it is inevitable that we will eventually stop printing telephone books, opting instead for the ease of searching and instant updates of online electronic databases, so too will most real estate listings eventually be offered predominantly on the Internet. Not only can information on the property be listed, but information can be included on the area, school district, shopping facilities, and other amenities, as well as an analysis of the investment.

Keeping Your Eyes Peeled

A great source of deals is simply to keep your eyes wide open as you go about your daily business. A handmade "For Sale" sign at least opens up the possibility that the owner is trying to sell the property himself without the commission expense of a real estate firm, and therefore without such a firm's expertise as to what the property may be worth. Of course a "For Sale by Owner" sign is a giveaway that there is no agent involved. The significance of this is not that the involvement of an agent is undesirable from a buyer's perspective (on the contrary, they can provide useful information such as recent comparable sales, known as "comps"; market trends; and suggestions as to what to do with the property). Rather, it is that in trying to save maybe 6 percent agent's commission, the seller is showing that he is willing to risk selling at way below market value.

Apart from "For Sale" signs, you may also notice "For Lease" signs on buildings. If the building has been available for lease for a long time, then the owner may be ready to give up on finding a tenant and instead feel forced to sell. You, in turn, may be able to buy the property for a great price, knowing that you can more easily find a tenant.

Often you will see a sign that says "For Sale or Lease." This, of course, is a dead giveaway that the owner is nearing his wits' end, as he cannot easily find a tenant or buyer, and is willing to settle for either—whichever comes along first. There may well be a great opportunity here to acquire a bargain.

Another benefit of driving around is that in addition to "For Sale" signs, "For Lease" signs, and "For Sale or Lease" signs, you will see properties without any signs but which look as though the owner would be grateful for any offer. I am talking about buildings that look derelict, where the grass is overgrown, trash is blown up against the fences, the windows are all covered in layers of dust, and there are weeds in the driveways and parking areas. These owners don't even have the motivation to put up a "For Sale" sign! Go to the county assessor's office, land transfer office, or whatever it is called where you live, look up who the registered owner is, and contact them to see if they are willing to sell. Nine out of ten may be offended by the intrusion, but the tenth may thank you for making him an offer—even a low one.

Keeping your eyes open for potential deals pays big dividends. In this regard, if you commute between your home and an office, or if you take kids to school every day, or if you have other destinations that you drive to regularly, do not take the same route each time. That would be as boring as having the same hotel room in the same location for each annual vacation. You could be missing out on a great "For Sale by Owner" deal one block over from your normal, seen-it-a-thousand-times-before route.

Years ago I was running a mentoring program for a dozen people. One participant was a Samoan chap who lamented to me on the very first day that his chances of success in real estate were very limited, as he was so hard up that he was working two shifts driving a taxi cab for 16 hours a day, and by the time he had eaten, slept, and said hello to his family, there was no time left over to start looking at real estate deals.

"No time to start looking at real estate deals?" I asked incredulously. "You don't know how lucky you are! You get to spend sixteen hours a day driving around town looking at new deals on the market. You will be one of the first to know where all the new 'For Sale' signs are. You get to talk with dozens of people each day, some of whom will be in the industry. Use your eyes, ears, and mouth, and you will soon be on your way." With this new per-spective on his situation, he ended up finding deal after deal, and eventually brought many family members into his growing real estate empire. So if you think it is difficult for you to drive around looking for deals, maybe you should become a taxi driver for a while to get a new perspective on things.

Networking

While I was living in Christchurch, New Zealand, I would get to-gether once a week for an early breakfast with a bunch of eager people involved in some aspect of real estate. We had a real estate agent, a financier, a leasing agent, and a few keen people wanting to break into real estate, all contributing ideas, contacts, listings, and generous doses of enthusiasm. There is an old but true saying that you become the company you keep. If you hang with people who think that the world owes them a living, that the government should pay them more money for doing nothing, and that all wealthy people must be sinister, then you will start to lose your creativity. Fire some of your friends every now and then so that you surround yourself only with positive, upbeat people. Remem-ber, you become the company you keep!

Word of Mouth

Looking at advertisements, surfing the Internet, and driving around town looking for deals, while valid methods of finding real estate for sale, are not necessarily the ultimate methods of sourcing great deals. The best method, in my experience, is what comes to you through word-of-mouth. If you tell enough people that you are on the lookout for great real estate deals, and if you remind them of this often enough and with sufficient enthusiasm, then deals will come your way with monotonous regularity.

You may think that your Uncle Tom could not possibly help you in your career. After all, he sells health insurance, so what could he possibly know about commercial real estate? If you tell him what you are up to (buying judiciously priced commercial real estate) and that you are always on the lookout for new opportunities, he may not come up with 10 deals for you before dinner that night, but you may just get a phone call in the months ahead from a friend of Uncle Tom's dentist, who heard about your endeavors and has a proposition for you.

Soon after moving to Phoenix I took a visiting investor from Australia to La Grande Orange, an upbeat eatery down the road from our offices (who, incidentally, leases office space in one of our buildings). I was talking with this visitor while waiting to place our order, when a man, overhearing our accents, commented that it was not common to hear two Australians talking in Phoenix. Of course I had to point out that the two Australians were my visitor and himself, for I was definitely not Australian, but rather a New Zealander.

Anyway, the interjector, Adrian Heyman, joined us for lunch. It turned out that he was a real estate agent with uncommonly good connections to bankers who deal with the inappropriately named real estate owned (REO) properties. They should be called *bank-owned*, as the bank has foreclosed on them and taken them back, although BO is probably not a good acronym. Perhaps REO is short for *real estate owned by banks*. Anyway, Adrian also has an uncommonly good sense of humor, despite his misfortune of being born on the wrong side of the Tasman

Sea. We started looking at deals around town, became good friends, and now attend each others' children's birthday parties. You never know where your next lead is going to come from. Be open to possibilities, be interested in what others have to say, and be interesting, otherwise you will be dumped on the scrap heap of indifference.

Early on in my negotiations with the National Association of Realtors (NAR) when they were first looking at endorsing one of my books,[2] the woman I was primarily dealing with phoned me to say her grandfather had 80 acres of land in Tonopah, Arizona, that he wanted to sell, and asked if I had any interest. Think about this. She was part of the management team that had, at the time, 1.2 million real estate agents as members (there are more now), and yet she asked *me* if I had any interest in her grandfather's land. Let people know what you are doing with enthusiasm and pride, and people will beat a path to your door to catch some of your energy.

Just how do you let people know what you do? First, watch less television, talk a bit more, and listen a lot more. Furthermore, take out your business card right now, and study it. I mean it, take it out right now! I know that 99 out of 100 people have their name in bold, large letters, and underneath, in smaller letters, is an official sounding title such as "Senior Vice President" or "Southern Regional Rep." These lofty-sounding titles can be as ridiculous as "dust relocation engineer" for house cleaner. For a while when signing my name to official documents requiring a title, I would put, "Chief Assistant to the Junior Clerk." Most people were so impressed with the sound of it they failed to register the meaning.

---

[2]At the time of this writing, the NAR has endorsed two of my books—the only books that they have endorsed to date.

Well, dang it all, how are people going to know that you are ready, willing, and able to buy commercial real estate if your card is like 99 out of 100?

The first thing you have to do is change your title to "Commercial Real Estate Investor," or, if you want to be a bit more daring, "Commercial Real Estate Deal Maker." The second thing is you must realize that no one other than your mother and a handful of other people are going to be interested in your name. So instead of having a card like this:

David Smith

Commercial Real Estate Investor

Phone (555) 123-4567
Fax (555) 765-4321
Email David@smith.com

Try something more like this:

David Smith

Commercial Real Estate Investor

Phone (555) 123-4567
Fax (555) 765-4321
Email David@smith.com

Furthermore, you may put a tagline on the card to explain what you do, as follows:

David Smith

Commercial Real Estate Investor

Phone (555) 123-4567
Fax (555) 765-4321
Email David@smith.com

I buy commercial buildings, vacant or tenanted.

The benefits of having business cards with your title of Commercial Real Estate Investor emblazoned across it, and a tagline to explain what you do, are twofold. First, it obviously lets everyone who receives your card know exactly what it is you do. Compared with your previous cards, this is a huge step in the right direction! Knowing that you are the southern regional rep will no sooner bring forth a commercial real estate deal than it will an offer of a free ticket to an Elton John concert.

The second benefit is that each time you give out a card, it reminds *you* of what you do. It reinforces in your mind the fact that you are truly a commercial real estate investor. Even if you are just getting started, still put "Commercial Real Estate Investor" and not "Budding Investor," "Would Be If I Could Be Investor," "Intending, Hoping, and Praying to be an Investor," or anything like that. You simply state that you are a commercial real estate investor. In this manner, you will infuse the notion into your subconscious mind, which will help manifest this reality in your life.

Letting people know what it is you do is a crucial step to achieving your goals. To further enhance your chances of having people help you on your way, why not print something like this on the back of your business card:

$1,000 reward given for information
leading to the acquisition
of an investment property.

Chances are that many people, on hearing that you invest in commercial real estate, will think the entire topic is way over their heads, and will therefore not even think to offer you any leads. However, to these same people, $1,000 may be a sufficiently large sum to entice them to keep a vigilant lookout for you. If the storage facility down the road from them comes on the market, they may just phone you. If they see that the gas station on the corner near where their aunt lives is for sale, they may e-mail you. Let people know what you do, and give them every reason and opportunity to contact you.

I will never forget traveling to Los Angeles to run a seminar some years ago. The event was being held at a hotel close to LAX airport. When I was driven through the car park to the lobby, I noticed a large parked van with "We Buy Real Estate, Phone (555) 123-4567" emblazoned in foot-high letters on both sides of the vehicle. During the seminar, I made reference to this van, and asked how many people in the audience had noticed it. Nearly every person in the room put up a hand. I then asked for the owner to come to a microphone. I asked him if the sign worked for him, and through an enormous grin he said something like, "It works astoundingly well." I asked him why he was grinning, and his response was, "It works so well that frankly I cannot understand why more people do not do this. I'm a bit scared that after tonight everyone will do this and we'll lose our competitive advantage."

People often come up to me and ask me to help them make a fortune in real estate. They claim they have been trying really hard but have not managed to make any headway. I ask to see their business cards, which are usually nondescript with their names in a large font and a nondescript title. No wonder they haven't made any headway! And how arrogant of them to expect me to drop everything I am doing to help them, when they are not even willing to let other people (let alone themselves) know what it is they do.

So get on the phone or Internet and order yourself some new business cards. If you are really cheap, there are many outfits on the Internet that will print them free for you.

Maybe this will be a good indication of your dedication to commercial real estate: Will you, within a few days, have a new set of business cards? They need not necessarily replace your existing cards, which you may need to keep for your work or other purposes. However, there is nothing wrong with having a second set that you use for all real estate–related activities.

Helping Other People

A few years back, I ran a three-day real estate investment seminar at the Arizona Biltmore Hotel. It is a beautiful hotel, inspired in part by famed architect Frank Lloyd Wright, and it suits me in particular because it is walking distance from my home. We had a great turnout at this seminar, with investors coming from as far away as Australia, Hong Kong, and Ireland.

On the third day, we ran a bus tour all over Phoenix, showing properties that were for sale that illustrated the topics that had been discussed in the previous two days. While the buses were stopped at a water-ski lake development similar to the one that I am involved with through Best Choice Properties, a participant from Ireland by the name of Ian Jackson walked up to me as I was finishing a call on my cell phone, and asked in his thick Irish brogue whether I liked the Sony Ericsson. Yes, I said, I did, but I was bothered by one thing. It was, by all accounts, Sony Ericsson's top-of-the-line PDA phone, and had Bluetooth built in. Similarly, I had the top-of-the-line Lexus automobile with the ultra luxury kit, also with Bluetooth built in. And yet my top-of-the-line phone couldn't talk with my top-of-the-line car. We chuckled about this, and must have discussed other matters; before long the bus tour continued, and that night the event was over.

Three weeks later, I received a brown box in the mail at the office. Being busy, and having no clue as to who it was from, I left it till the end of the day, when I thought I had better open it to find out what was inside. To my surprise, it was a brand-new Sony Ericsson, the then-latest Sony PDA phone and successor to my model, which worked smoothly and first time with my Lexus, compliments of Ian Jackson.

A few months later I ran an event in Birmingham, England, and there was Ian Jackson again, with his son Tim. Thereafter Ian would turn up in Phoenix, doing deals and attending courses, usually with one or more family members in tow. We would meet for dinner, talk about real estate, the joy of having kids, and the meaning of life, and over time we became friends.

One day Ian phoned me and said that he was involved with a company in the United Kingdom that provided leads on residential properties that could be acquired for around 75 percent of market value. It was called A Quick Sale (www.AQuickSale.co.uk), and Ian had told the owners that he knew me and that we should all get together. Despite some initial disbelief that Ian did in fact know me, the owners of the company duly came out to the United States, and we got to brainstorming. The net effect was that I ended up speaking at their national conference in the United Kingdom in December of that year. While speaking, I touched on the merits of commercial real estate, and this inspired the franchisees of A Quick Sale to lobby the owners to set up a commercial franchise network (up until then the organization was entirely residential). And so, in the following March, I opened the commercial division of A Quick Sale in Coventry with a two-day conference on commercial real estate.

Ian Jackson had been buying up more franchises in the United Kingdom, and now we are discussing how we may get involved in the U.S. side of the operation.

The point behind all of this is that being friendly, kind, and encouraging toward others is not something to be embarrassed about. Rather, great friendships and business relations can be formed from the most simple of meetings. Have an open mind, be kind, be fair, be curious, be cautious, be adventurous, do some good, teach a little, learn a little, make some money, give some of it away, and cherish the friends you make along the way.

The 100:10:3:1 Rule

Patience and perseverance seem to be qualities that are not easy to find these days. I am stunned at the number of people who attend a seminar or read some of my writings, and then contact my office two weeks later and complain, "I looked for a great deal for two weeks and haven't found anything! Help me out!"

So let me spell out one of my fundamental rules, the 100:10:3:1 rule. This rule simply states that you must look at 100 properties to find 10 that you may want to submit an offer on. Submitting 10 offers does not mean that 10 offers are accepted (if all 10 were accepted, then in general you would know that you are offering too much). Of the 10 offers submitted, maybe only 3 are accepted.

Similarly, having three accepted offers does not mean that you can go ahead and buy all three properties. You still have to complete due diligence (more on this in Chapter 11) and arrange finance (see Chapter 13). Maybe you can only close on one of the three accepted offers.

The net result is that you will have looked at 100 properties in order to buy just one. And if you didn't buy any out of the 100 you looked at, then you would have to look at another 100 to have a decent chance of ending up buying one of those.

In other words, finding a suitable property is a numbers game. If you expect to be able to go out and look at two or three commercial properties, and as a result find one that suits you, can be bought at a good price, is cash flow positive, and has good growth potential, then you are dreaming. It may happen with the first property you look at, but by the same token you may look at 100 or even 200 and not find one that suits you. That is where the patience and perseverance I mentioned come in.

By the way, the numbers 100, 10, 3, and 1 are not simply pulled out of thin air. In my personal experience, and that of countless associates and students, these are about the ratios that work for both beginners and experienced investors. The challenge is not that there is a shortage of deals out there. Rather, the challenge is that there is a shortage of patience, determination, perseverance, focus, and, dare I say it, sacrifice, to find them.

What typically happens is that a budding investor, armed with newfound knowledge of the 100:10:3:1 rule, optimistically goes out into the market to look at 100 properties, thereby thinking he will be guaranteed to end up buying one. During the first week, he manages to look at six properties, and during the following week, he manages to consider eight. Being the optimist he is, he pulls out his calculator, and works out that at this rate he should own a building within three months. So far, so good.

During the third week, however, he has to attend his cousin's engagement party; the following week it is raining; the week after, he has a bit of a cold and is out of action for a couple of days and not feeling too good for the rest of the week. The week after that, he is on a retreat with work; the week after, he is so engrossed in a computer game that he forgets to feed his cat, let alone look at property; and the next week he throws up his hands and declares, to himself as much as anyone else, that the silly 100:10:3:1 rule simply doesn't work. While this scenario may seem contrived, I know the result is true: Most people do not have the singular focus of looking at deal after deal after deal after deal, to find their needle in the haystack, even when they know that the deal of the decade comes along about once a week.

Oddly enough, these same people can muster tremendous personal resources to make sure that they get to see their weekly soap or reality show (and the patience to put up with an average of around 15 minutes of advertisements per hour while they watch television). They demonstrate perseverance in regularly spending a lot of time on their favorite social networking web sites, looking at the inane personal information of complete strangers. They are willing to sacrifice time with their loved ones to drink with people they barely know. They show tremendous determination in acquiring scalped tickets to the next basketball game. But often, when it comes to looking at real estate, these same qualities of resourcefulness, patience, perseverance, sacrifice, and determination are buried under a notion that acquiring real estate is simply too difficult.

Most men spend more time deciding which car to get next than they do looking for a piece of income-generating real estate. These men will read consumer reports and car magazines, talk with their buddies, test-drive countless vehicles, compare options, consider brake/horsepower ratings and the number of seconds taken to reach 60 mph, talk with salesmen, and spend countless hours conducting research on the Internet, all to buy a car that will cost money to own and operate, and that will depreciate during the few brief years of ownership. After two or three years, they go through this entire process again to buy their next car. And yet they do not make any time to look for an investment vehicle that only needs to be bought once and will generate income, appreciate, and feed them *forever*.

Women, in general, do not dissipate as much energy choosing a new car. Last week my nanny, Kim, turned up in a new VW. When I asked her how it came about, she replied that she wasn't really looking for a car that day, but when she saw it, she just loved it and had to have it. Of course if women devoted all the time they saved choosing a vehicle to finding commercial real estate, then there would be a lot more wealthy female real estate investors. Rather, they have their own passions that they like to devote time to, which I would probably be wise not to comment on.

The point is, no one is going to walk up and hand you the title of a great commercial deal on a silver platter. To acquire income-generating real estate, you have to make the effort to look for, find, negotiate, and finance deals. Every human being on this planet has one thing in common: We all have 24 hours to spend each day. How you spend your time each day will help determine the rest of your life.

Summary

When you accept that you have to look at a lot of properties to find one that is suitable for you, you have the mind-set to succeed. When you study the "Commercial Real Estate for Sale" section in the newspapers, monitor listings on the Internet, keep in regular contact with a selection of real estate agents, keep your eyes peeled for potential properties for sale, have business cards that announce what you do more prominently than what you are called, and put the word out that you are in the market to acquire properties, the deals will start to flow faster than you can analyze them. Clearly, we will need a fast and efficient way of determining if a property is a good investment—the topic of our next chapter.

CHAPTER 11

Analyzing Deals

Think back to my wet fish supply shop in Chapter 10. The asking price was $59,000, and the triple-net lease had an annual income of $10,400, resulting in a return on investment (ROI) of 17.63 percent. When faced with an opportunity like this, what else is left to analyze? I had seen the building. It was old—maybe 50 years old—but it was in sound condition. The business had been around for years, so it had a proven track record. I was happy and confident to sign the purchase contract without so much as pulling out a calculator.

Not all commercial real estate deals are this clear-cut. This one was particularly small, had a single tenant, and was therefore simple to figure out, even in your head.

More realistically, a commercial building may be on numerous titles, all with different encumbrances, plot ratios, and recession planes. There may be 25 separately leasable premises, with tenants on leases in 19 of them, month-to-month tenants in another four, and vacancies in the remaining two premises. Lease terms may vary from tenant to tenant, rentals per square foot may be different, and some tenancies may include parking while others have to pay extra for it. There may be three existing mortgages on the property, with only two being assumable. Clearly, it would be daring to sign up for such a property on the spot without doing a bit of work.

So just what do you need to find out? And is there a method to quickly analyze a deal to know if it is worth pursuing?

Due Diligence

With commercial real estate, reference is often made to undertaking *due diligence*. Generally, due diligence refers to the care a reasonable person should take before entering into an agreement or a transaction with another party. More specifically, as it relates to real estate, due diligence simply means finding out enough about a property to make sure it is a good deal. This includes reviewing all financial records plus anything else relevant to the property that could affect your decision as to whether you should buy it.

One of the first steps when doing due diligence is to make sure that the seller is in fact the legal owner or representative of the property being offered for sale. The following examples highlight how crucial this is.

The Eiffel Tower was originally built for the World Exhibition in Paris in 1889. (See Figure 11.1.) Named after its famed designer, Gustave Eiffel, the tower was intended to be demolished at the end of the Expo. However, Parisians had been so impressed with the new iconic symbol gracing their city and the astounding views that could be enjoyed from its highest observation level,

Figure 11.1   **The Eiffel Tower, Sold Twice without Due Diligence**

that it was decided to let it continue to overlook the City of Love. It was, after all, the tallest structure in the world, and remained so until 1930.

In May 1925, however, a small article appeared in a Paris newspaper that claimed the Eiffel Tower was in dire need of repair as the iron was rusting. The cost of the repair was prohibitive, and there was a brief comment that the government was exploring the idea of tearing it down rather than repairing it.

Subsequently, letters were sent to five scrap iron dealers on official government letterhead, inviting them to a hotel suite to discuss a possible government contract. At this meeting an official made the announcement that the government had indeed decided to scrap the Eiffel Tower, and asked for bids to be tendered for its sale, demolition, and scrap metal salvage. The official added that since it was such a controversial move, the men had to remain quiet regarding the tower's fate or risk dramatic public protests.

Within four days, all of the dealers submitted their bids. The winner, André Poisson, was notified and he promptly paid.

There was only one problem. While the newspaper article discussing the state of the tower had been real, the letters to the iron dealers were fake. They were the work of notorious confidence trickster Count Victor Lustig, who had forged the letterheads and played the role of the government official. When asked by one of the dealers why, since this was a government contract, the meeting was being held in a hotel suite, he answered that it was all part of the elaborate plan to keep the information from the public for as long as possible.

On receiving the payment of the winning bid, Count Lustig fled to Zurich, where he read all the Paris daily newspapers, waiting for the story of his con to hit. It never did. Lustig concluded that André Poisson was too embarrassed to own up to falling for the con—so he returned to Paris, and, incredibly, sold the Eiffel Tower for a second time.[1]

I, too, have been caught out by a failure to conduct sufficient due diligence on the ownership of a property. I had bought a building in Phoenix zoned for restricted commercial use. The zoning was slated for a change to general commercial use, which to me made the property more interesting. One day I was taking a busload of Australian investors on a tour of Phoenix, and we all got out of the bus to look at this property. With all these people as witnesses, the owner of the property next door came over, identified himself, and announced that he owned 10 feet of the land on my side of the fence and that he wanted it back straight away, so the fence would have to be shifted and, further, all my buildings on his land would have to be demolished.

Initially I wrote him off as someone trying to take me for a ride. I asked why, if he owned a strip 10 feet wide, the fence, driveways, curbing, and landscaping all indicated that the boundary was where the fence was. He had some convoluted explanation of unpaid back taxes by the previous owner of my property, and an agreement to carve off 10 feet and give it to this neighbor in return for him paying off the back taxes. I asked him why the selling agent had not told me of this, and he replied that he had repeatedly tried to explain the situation to her and supply

---

[1] After this sale, the police were on to him, and Lustig fled back to the United States. He continued his cons but died in Alcatraz in 1947, broke, at the age of 57.

her with supporting documentation so that she could fairly represent the facts, but that she had dismissed him as a fool and literally told him not to bother her again. In terms of entertainment for my students, I could not have orchestrated a more amusing situation.

The neighbor gave me his attorney's card and invited me to speak with him or check the title with the Maricopa County records. I did both. It turns out he was absolutely right. The title clearly showed a 10-foot strip of land under separate ownership which, equally clearly, I had not bought. (See Figure 11.2.)

Needless to say, this should have been revealed by the seller. Failing that, it should have been uncovered and revealed by the selling agent, especially in the light of her arrogant dismissal of the neighbor. It probably should have been uncovered by my buyer's agent, and by the title company. No one admitted any responsibility, and they all pointed the proverbial finger at the other participants to this transaction.

I contacted the broker for the selling agent, and he came back and told me that the selling agent claimed she never once spoke with the neighbor. He added that he was a veteran broker and an expert witness in court cases, and that I wouldn't stand a chance with any court action.

This thinly veiled attempt to discourage me from pursuing any litigation has nothing whatsoever to do with my decision not to take any legal action. Rather, I am averse to battling things out through attorneys, as often they are the ones who end up with all the money, and you may still not get the outcome that is right.

Instead, I talked with the neighbor, found out he was in some considerable financial difficulty, and ended up buying the 10-foot

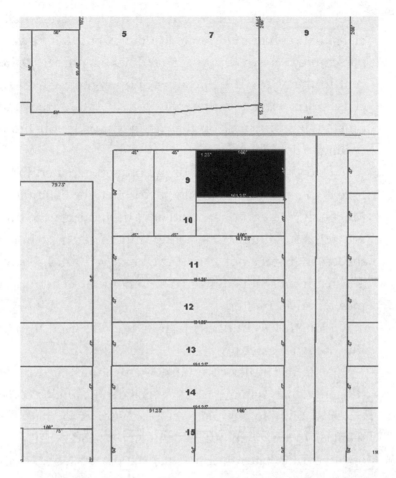

Figure 11.2 **Subject Lot (Shown in Black) with 10-Foot Strip on South Border**

strip of land from him for around half of what my attorney told me it would probably cost to take it through the courts (with an outcome that was still not guaranteed).

This strategy of avoiding aggressive confrontations and seeking solutions that have benefits for everyone may have a few disadvantages at times, but overall it works in your favor. This past week, the same neighbor contacted me and stated that his financial situation had deteriorated to the extent that he was filing for bankruptcy. He was tipping me off that his property (the one adjacent to mine) could be acquired, no longer for his original purchase price or even its present appraisal, but for the amount of his outstanding principal on the mortgage, or less if the bank were willing to do a short sale.

Had the selling agent of my property treated him like a human being, maybe she would have gotten the listing for his house. Maybe she or her broker could have been the ones to buy his property for around half of its market value. They have not yet learned the lesson that it's not *who's* right, but *what's* right. Their arrogance and fear of loss has delivered yet another buying opportunity to me on a silver platter.

Nonetheless, it does illustrate the dire need to conduct your due diligence carefully.

Note that sellers can (and often should) also perform a due diligence analysis on the buyer. The main thing to consider is the buyer's ability to complete the purchase, as the last thing a seller wants is to accept an offer from a buyer, send other potential buyers away, and later find out that the purchaser was not good for the purchase price.

Two categories need to be considered as part of the due diligence. The first comprises items that, in general, cannot be quantified. We are talking about general street appeal (important for retail space and some office space, but less important for warehouses); whether the property is on the edge of a floodplain; whether there is good freeway access nearby; how close the property is to a trunk railway line, airport, or seaport (these factors may be more relevant for a warehouse); or the demographics of passing foot traffic (this could be relevant to retail space).

Also included in this category are items that may be quantified, but where it is difficult to know what to do with the numbers. For instance, you may find out that foot traffic averages 600 pedestrians per hour, or that there are 32,000 cars going by on average every day, but just what do you do with that information? Similarly, you may want to know what high-speed Internet access options are available (DSL signals deteriorate the farther you are from a telephone exchange, cable Internet requires that physical cables are already in the area, and wireless Internet services do not work equally well everywhere). But just what do you do with the information that there is no cable, and DSL can deliver a maximum download speed of 1.5Mbps?

Fortunately, most of these items will already be taken care of in the market rentals and cap rates for that particular area. Properties with great freeway access, high foot-traffic volumes, and fast Internet capacity will generally attract a higher rental than comparable buildings without these features. Similarly, cap rates will generally be lower, as investors are willing to accept a lower return, knowing that in the event of a tenant not renewing a lease (or going bankrupt) it will be easier to attract a new tenant to an appealing building with great qualitative features.

Note that the appeal of some features changes with time. For instance, as an increasing proportion of goods are transported and distributed by air as opposed to by sea (both domestically and internationally), the relative value of a warehouse with close and easy access to a busy airport will go up, while a warehouse near a soon-to-be-closed railway station or an aging and seldom-used port will decline. Of course, if you have a warehouse near the port of Long Beach, Rotterdam, or Singapore, rentals will remain high as these ports continue to be very busy.

The point is, you have to be aware of features and trends that go beyond numbers that you can enter into a calculator. It is precisely because many of these items are difficult to quantify that many purchasers do not bother to consider them.

While I cannot offer you a formula to evaluate commercial real estate based on qualitative aspects (unlike the next category, where I do have a formula), I encourage you to become aware of trends in your neighborhood, your city, your province or state, your country, and globally, because keeping abreast of what is happening can prevent some costly blunders and can also lead you to some spectacular deals. Read books like Thomas Friedman's *The Lexus and the Olive Tree* (Farrar, Straus & Giroux, 1999) and his more recent *The World Is Flat* (Farrar, Straus & Giroux, 2005) to find out how the world is evolving. Study *The Sovereign Individual*, by James Davidson and William Rees-Mogg (Simon & Schuster, 1997), to find out about what they call the "coming economic revolution." We live in an exciting age. Become a participant and, if you are really bold, help shape it.

The second category of items that need to be considered as part of the due diligence process comprises all the facts and figures related to the property. The seller or his agent may claim that the total land area is 38,000 square feet, or that the net rentable area is 9,850 square meters, or that the present rent roll is $126,000, or that property taxes are $20,817, or that the lease has another 12 years to run, but you would be foolish to rely on someone else's research, recollection, or assumptions.

Once, I was looking at a block of retail shops in downtown San Diego, and the seller claimed a handsome ROI of 15 percent. Early on in the due diligence process, however, I discovered that the actual ROI was only a comparatively paltry 9 percent. When I pointed out this dramatic difference to the seller, he merely shrugged his shoulders and said, "Well it is still a very good deal!

You should see how fast buildings are appreciating around here." I have no idea whether this was a genuine mistake or a contrived method to boost the apparent returns and thus lure a buyer who opted not to check the figures, but it does highlight the importance of conducting your own due diligence.[2]

Part of the due diligence, then, is to confirm or establish what certain key financial figures are, such as rental income, property taxes, management fees, elevator service contract fees, other maintenance fees, and lease durations.

However, it is one thing to determine or verify what certain key figures are. It is another thing altogether to know what to do with these numbers. Most beginners in commercial real estate are so keen to consummate their first deal, that just about all they will look at is the ROI. Full of enthusiasm, they will point out that they can buy a $1 million property with an ROI of 9 percent, and since the mortgage they have lined up is only costing 8.5 percent, they are ready to sign a contract there and then, because surely the property must be cash flow positive, so what could possibly go wrong?

Well, here is one scenario of how you could lose out. Let's say you pay $1 million for this building, and you are happily collecting your $90,000 a year in rent. One day, to your horror, you discover that the tenant is no longer there. He may have skipped town (and you would then face hefty costs in trying to track him down), or there may have been a clause in the lease (that you did not study as part of your due diligence) that left him off the hook if his franchisor went out of business, or perhaps the lease expired (and you had foolishly taken the seller's word at face value that

---

[2]A 9 percent return in downtown San Diego was—and still is—very good. My decision not to proceed was based on the building not meeting earthquake code.

the lease still had a decade to run). So far, there is no real problem, as you have already learned how to attract a new tenant. However, to your further horror, you discover that market rents in the area for the size of building you have are only $40,000 a year, not the $90,000 that the previous tenant was paying. Suddenly it dawns on you that you may have been set up—an artificially high rent was put in place between the seller and an accomplice for the sole purpose of luring you into paying way too much for a building.

Four Questions to Ask about Any Commercial Property

Consequently, when you are looking at any commercial property, I encourage you to ask the following four questions:

1. What rent is being achieved in the subject property?
2. What are market rentals in the area?
3. What does the building cost per square foot or meter to buy?
4. What is the replacement cost per square foot or meter?

Clearly you need to establish what the true rents are at present. This may require some study of the lease. Apart from the tactic previously described to artificially raise the rent, there could be a deal between the landlord and the tenant whereby the rental during the first year was free, in return for a greater-than-market rent in subsequent years.

In addition to establishing the actual rents being collected on the property, you need to determine what market rents are. If, for instance, the actual rent is $15 per square foot (psf) but market rents are only $10 psf, then on the surface this may seem like a great deal (you would be collecting more than the market is willing to offer), but in reality this is a problem. For one, the higher-than-market rent has already been capped out by the cap rate to give a high capital value—higher than it should be based on market rentals. Should you lose your tenant, then you would in all probability not attract a new tenant for anything more than $10 psf, and the capital value would fall by one-third. Further, it will be a long time before you can ever invoke a rent increase (market rents would have to rise from $10 psf to over $15 psf), thereby limiting for quite some time the growth in capital value of your property.

Conversely, if the actual rent collected is the same $15 psf, but market rents are $20 psf, then this works in your favor. First, you will probably be able to acquire the property at a discount to its true market value, as it is the $15 psf that is being divided by the market cap rate, and not $20 psf. Second, at the next rent review, you know that you can increase the rental by a full 33 percent to bring it up to market levels, thereby increasing the value of the property by the same 33 percent.

As we mentioned in Chapter 8, increasing the rent by 33 percent will open you up to accusations by tenants of being unfair, unscrupulous, and usurious. They will argue vociferously that a rental increase of a whopping 33 percent is unconscionable. However, when you point out to the tenants that market rents are in fact already $20 psf, and that you are not unfairly increasing the rent to what you see fit, but rather that they have enjoyed a substantial discount to market rentals for a long time, and you are simply bringing them (belatedly) up to market levels, they will realize how lucky they have been. Most will accept that if they had to rent premises elsewhere, they would have to pay $20 psf, so they will be quite happy knowing they had a long-term discount that has come to an unfortunate end.

Similarly, question 3 asks what the building costs per square foot or meter to buy, so that we can compare that to (question 4) what a new building would cost. If you are paying $2 million for a building and the replacement cost is $3 million, that is likely to be a good deal, as the difference could be accounted for by wear and tear and depreciation. However, if you are paying $2 million for a building, and the replacement cost is only $1 million, then you have to wonder why you don't simply go out and build a new one.

So if the rents being collected on a property are below market levels, and the building is costing less than the cost of a new one, then things are, so far, looking good.

Return on Investment

The concept of return on investment, or ROI, is probably the most common indicator used to determine if a property is a good deal. However, there are many flavors to the ROI.

For instance, if we define the ROI as the rental income divided by purchase price, do we mean *gross income* or *net income*? And if we are talking about net income, do we mean net *pretax* income or net *after-tax* income? And is the servicing of a mortgage taken into account as one of the expenses? After all, what is the point of a 10 percent return if interest rates are 11 percent?

My challenge with all the variations on ROI that I have seen brokers use is twofold. First off, each investor has a different set of circumstances (cash in bank, creditworthiness, contacts to attract tenants, resources to implement zone changes, etc.); therefore, a property with an ROI of 10 percent may be appropriate for one investor and totally inappropriate for another. Further, the ROI is just a snapshot of how the property is performing *in that instant*—it takes no account at all of what will happen in the future.

What I want is more than a snapshot of what is happening now. I want a *movie into the future*. To help me create it, I relied on the following words of wisdom:

> *The reasonable person accepts the world the way it is. The un-reasonable person insists on changing the world to suit his own devices. That is why all progress depends on unreason-able people.*

I had been playing around with spreadsheets and automated analyses for years, and teamed up with various people to create ways of analyzing real estate for both my own use and that of students and clients. These tools, while functional, were not always compelling. However, in June 2000, I met a Polish programmer in Osaka, Japan, who lived in Australia with his Thai wife. He demonstrated some of his software programs to me and, seeing the brilliance of his programming, I unreasonably asked him to create my movie. When he asked me how soon I wanted it, I answered jokingly, "In six weeks' time!" Rather than taking it as joke, he pondered for a brief moment and then said it would probably involve a few late nights, but got to work nonetheless.

My background in electrical engineering no doubt helped me be able to specify exactly what I wanted and, to a certain extent, to speak the same language as this computer programmer who was as unreasonable as I was.

Six weeks later, in time for my annual tour of Australia, we had the first incarnation of our now renowned Real Estate Acquisition Program (REAP) software. In the ensuing seven years,

REAP has been refined, streamlined, and enhanced to the point where it has become the software of choice for serious investors all over the world. It is the software I developed and use to analyze my projects to determine their financial viability. As a commercial investor yourself, you need some sort of system or program to analyze your potential projects.

The REAP software incorporates my 30 years of experience in real estate. It condenses what I know about real estate, extracts the pertinent quantifiable figures relevant to a property, massages the numbers in a logical way, and presents them in a way that lets investors know whether a particular property is *suitable to them* as an investment, taking into account their specific circumstances. The reports generated by REAP also serve to help secure mortgage funding, obtain a good valuation or appraisal, and attract equity partners to a deal. Being a movie rather than a snapshot, REAP appeals to all but the most stoic of investor personalities.

The software is designed to serve one purpose: to help you decide whether to buy a property. It is not a management package, trend analyzer, or defaulting tenant debt collector.

Most beginner investors scribble down numbers on the back of an envelope to work out ratios, or enter numbers into a calculator. The challenge is that if they repeat the exercise, they will likely get a different result, as the second time around they forget to put in the vacancy rate, or the management fees, or the property taxes. Good software overcomes this by prompting for every relevant detail each time.

As with any piece of software, the results are governed by the acronym GIGO—garbage in, garbage out. In other words, the more accurate the information you provide, the more accurate the results.

Here's an example of how to use a program to analyze your prospective property and see into the future. Assume you are considering buying a property for $10 million with a cash component of $1 million (the rest of the purchase price will be financed). Assume that in the first year, the pretax revenue (after expenses) is $502,480. The net ROI is 5.02 percent—the $502,480 of pretax income divided by the $10 million purchase price. This is the snapshot that I have referred to earlier. Remember, we want the movie.

An investment analysis report (see Figure 11.3) shows that while the pretax cash flow may be $502,480, the after-tax revenue is $447,606 (building and contents depreciation reduced the tax liability). Furthermore, in the subsequent four years, the after-tax revenues will be approximately $463,000, $481,000, $501,000, and $523,000. Not only that, but the equity at the end of five years will have increased to $7.9 million. Hold this thought.

Notice that the last line of the investment analysis reports the internal rate of return (IRR). The textbook definition of the IRR is technically correct and totally baffling, even to accountants: The IRR is the return that an investment would offer you, such that if you took all future revenues, and calculated their net present values, and added them all together, you would get a return equal to the cost of capital. (No, you don't need to remember this definition!)

In this example, we are putting $1 million cash into the property. In the first year, we are pulling out $447,606, in the next year $463,000, then $481,000, $501,000, and $523,000. We also note that at the end of five years, the equity in the property will have increased to $7.9 million.

The IRR is the return that a bank would have to give you, such that if you gave the bank the same $1 million, they could afford to give you $447,606 at the end of year one, $463,000 at the end of year two, $481,000 at the end of year three, $501,000 at the

Investment Analysis

The investment analysis report presents the results of all the main calculations supported by REAP. The following values are arranged in a logical order to allow easy visual interpretation and reference.

	Year 1	Year 2	Year 3	Year 4	Year 5
Renovations	0.00	0.00	0.00	0.00	0.00
Capital growth	9.00%	9.00%	9.00%	9.00%	9.00%
Property value	11,990,000.00	13,069,100.00	14,245,319.00	15,527,397.71	16,924,863.50
Loan amount	9,020,000.00	9,020,000.00	9,020,000.00	9,020,000.00	9,020,000.00
Equity	2,970,000.00	4,049,100.00	5,225,319.00	6,507,397.71	7,904,863.50
Inflation rate	3.00%	3.00%	3.00%	3.00%	3.00%
Gross rent	1,440,000.00	1,483,200.00	1,527,696.00	1,573,526.88	1,620,732.69
Principal repayment	0.00	0.00	0.00	0.00	0.00
Interest rate	7.60%	7.60%	7.60%	7.60%	7.60%
Loan interest	685,520.00	685,520.00	685,520.00	685,520.00	685,520.00
Additional repayment	0.00	0.00	0.00	0.00	0.00
Total loan payment	685,520.00	685,520.00	685,520.00	685,520.00	685,520.00
Special expenses	0.00	0.00	0.00	0.00	0.00
Total property expenses	252,000.00	259,560.00	267,346.80	275,367.20	283,628.22
Pretax cash flow	502,480.00	538,120.00	574,829.20	612,639.68	651,584.47
Pretax cash on cash	50.15%	53.70%	57.37%	61.14%	65.03%
Depreciation—Building	238,000.00	238,000.00	238,000.00	238,000.00	238,000.00
Depreciation—Contents	100,000.00	80,000.00	64,000.00	51,200.00	40,960.00
Total deductions	1,277,520.00	1,263,080.00	1,254,866.80	1,250,087.20	1,248,108.22
Tax credit	−54,874.02	−75,048.02	−93,496.24	−111,209.91	−128,424.58
After-tax cash flow	447,605.98	463,071.98	481,332.96	501,429.77	523,159.89
After-tax cash on cash	44.67%	46.21%	48.04%	50.04%	52.21%
Your income per week	8,607.81	8,905.23	9,256.40	9,642.88	10,060.77
Internal rate of return	435.72%	215.22%	158.35%	131.90%	116.73%

Figure 11.3   **Investment Analysis**

end of year four, and $523,000 at the end of year five. On top of that they would have to give you $7.9 million. To do so, a bank would have to offer you 116 percent interest.

The snapshot analysis shows gross ROI of 10 percent ($1 million of gross income divided by the purchase price of $10 million). This is what most brokers will tell you. I have no interest in this snapshot! What do I care how much the property costs? I certainly don't have to come up with $10 million, so in that sense the $10 million is irrelevant to me—it is only relevant in financing the deal.

You may also be told that the net return is 5.02 percent (the pretax revenue of $502,480 divided by the $10 million purchase price). While this is useful added information to the 10 percent gross return, it is still a snapshot of what is happening in that instant, and is still related to the $10 million purchase price.

All I care about is how much cash I have to put in, and how much cash I can pull out (or put in) each year, as well as the buildup in equity. That is the essence of my cash-flow transaction with the property. How much cash goes in, how much cash comes out, and how does the equity increase over time? That is our movie of the future.

The snapshot looks at today's rent and divides it by today's purchase price. Two properties could have the same current return of, say, 10 percent, even when one is in a declining market with declining rentals and capital values, and the other is in the fastest-growing market in the world. This is not very sophisticated analysis!

The movie looks at today's rent, to be sure, but also considers how those rents change over time. It acknowledges the purchase price, but it also considers the market value at the time of purchase, and then works out how the capital value changes over time according to the capital growth rate. The movie takes into account all acquisition expenses, and knows which can be deducted

for taxation purposes and which must be capitalized and depreciated. The movie takes into account all expenses associated with
the property, and how these change over time, and gives you a
net after-tax income figure for each year. By taking each year's net
after-tax income figure and combining it with the buildup in equity, you get to see how the property performs *over time*.

Once you are familiar with the movie, then hearing an agent
tell you that a property has an ROI of 10 percent will seem as useful as knowing that a car consumes about 20 gallons of gas per
tank. Knowing that the gas tank holds 20 gallons is perhaps of
some value, but surely you want to know the rate at which the gas
is consumed? Imagine asking your car dealer what the gas consumption was, because you felt that "20 gallons of gas per tank"
was insufficient information to decide if you wanted to buy the
car. Imagine that after much sighing and calculating, he comes up
with the answer, "I've got it! The car consumes three gallons per
hour!" Again, this is not the information you wanted. You would
now need to know at what speed the car was traveling to work out
what you really want to know, which is miles per gallon.[3]

The main reason I am not particularly interested in the ROI is
because it divides the rental income by the purchase price, and yet
the purchase price is about as useful to me as knowing how many
gallons of gas a tank holds. Let me illustrate this.

Imagine you have a choice between two commercial properties. The first has an income of $1 million, and can be bought for
$10 million with 10 percent cash. The second property also has an
income of $1 million, and can be bought for $20 million with 10
percent cash. Which one would you buy?

---

[3]Or kilometers per liter, or, as it is often expressed in the metric world, liters
per hundred kilometers.

Before dismissing this exercise as trivial, think very carefully. Clearly, on the basis of ROI alone, you would choose the $10 million property, as $1 million generated by a $10 million investment sounds better than $1 million generated by a $20 million investment. However, what if the $20 million property came with an assumable mortgage at 3 percent interest, whereas you could only raise financing at 8.7 percent for the $10 million property? Interest at 8.7 percent on a $9 million loan is $783,000, whereas 3 percent interest on an $18 million loan is only $540,000. After deducting mortgage interest, the return on the $10 million property is 2.17 percent ($217,000 divided by $10 million), whereas the return on the $20 million property is 2.3 percent ($460,000 divided by $20 million). Now which is the better deal?

Think this is too contrived? A former student and now friend, R.S. Schmitt, came to me with a property that was for sale in the Scottsdale Airpark. It was a large warehouse of some 44,000 square feet, and came with an assumable loan that was all of 0 percent for the first year, 1 percent for the second year, 2 percent for the third year, 3 percent for the fourth year, and 4 percent thereafter. If you don't think these opportunities exist, you will never find them, because even if one was presented to you on a proverbial silver platter, you would not believe it and would therefore dismiss the deal as a hoax.

Furthermore, in the comparison of the $10 million and $20 million properties, what if the first property had no fixtures or chattels that could be depreciated, whereas the second property came with chattels worth $8 million that could be depreciated at an average of 30 percent? Paying tax on $2.4 million less income (as a result of the depreciation allowance) could save $1.18 million in tax, assuming a 49 percent marginal tax rate. Your effective income would now be $2.18 million on the $20 million property

($1 million of rental income plus the $1.18 million of tax rebate), giving an effective ROI of nearly 11 percent, versus only 10 percent on the $10 million property.

Combining the mortgage interest and depreciation allowances, the $10 million property has a net income of $217,000, giving an ROI of 2.17 percent ($217,000 divided by $10 million) and a cash-on-cash return of 21.7 percent ($217,000 divided by $1 million). The $20 million property, however, has an effective net income of $1.64 million ($1 million of initial rental income, plus $1.18 million of depreciation rebate, less the $540,000 mortgage interest), giving an ROI of 8.2 percent ($1.64 million divided by $20 million) and a cash-on-cash return of 82 percent ($1.64 million divided by $2 million).

So *now* which is the better deal?

To further sway you from your initial reaction to buy the $10 million property, assume both properties were being offered at their respective market values. Since they both had rental incomes of $1 million, then market cap rates for the $10 million property must be 10 percent, and market cap rates for the $20 million property must be 5 percent. If both properties are subject to a 5 percent rental increase at the next rent review, then the rents go from $1 million to $1.05 million in both cases. However, with the $10 million building, that will only result in an increase in value of $500,000, whereas with the $20 million building, the same rent increase will result in an increase in value of $1 million.

Simply looking at a snapshot of the present rent and dividing it by the purchase price, while better than nothing, is not sufficiently sophisticated for you to make smart decisions as to which properties to buy. You need a tool that can quickly take all factors into account (such as mortgage interest and depreciation allowances) to work out the true effect on your returns.

It is, of course, impossible to expect any piece of software to give you a green or red light with regard to a property acquisition. Whether a deal is good depends largely on the circumstances of the investor. For instance, an investor with little cash but a lot of energy to put into a deal may be able to buy a high-yielding property that requires a bit of maintenance. Conversely, an investor with a lot of cash may be able to suffer a much lower return, in exchange for being able to buy a worry-free building in a more rapidly appreciating area.

After you have used software to analyze a couple of properties, you will find it difficult to revert back to analyzing properties with pencil and paper. Good software takes the emotion out of the decision as to whether you should buy the property. Furthermore, as Chapter 13 explains, you can include the reports from software with your proposal for financing to enhance the likelihood of obtaining mortgage funding, as the banker will be inclined to think, "Based on these numbers, it looks like a good deal."

Bear in mind that no software should make every deal look good. Rather, it should help you find great deals. Therefore, if a deal does not look good on paper when a banker is considering funding it, you probably don't want to buy the property anyway.

CHAPTER 12

Negotiating Commercial Real Estate Deals

Even when you have found many prospective investment properties and analyzed them to determine which you want to buy, there can still be a bit of work involved in actually acquiring them. You may have found a building with an asking price of $1 million. If you have the $1 million, in the form of either cash or a line of credit from a financial institution, then you could simply sign a contract to acquire the property, and you would own it. Usually, however, an acquisition takes more negotiation than that, as either you (the buyer) or the seller may want—or need—to haggle over the price, size of the down payment, interest rate on any carry-back loan, length of time that the seller guarantees the rental from month-to-month tenancies, and so forth.

There is a saying that you don't get what you deserve, you get what you negotiate. Clearly, an ability to negotiate will come in handy.

The Uncooperative Seller

Early one December I came across an advertisement in a local newspaper for a block of three shops for sale in a popular seaside resort. The advertisement quoted returns of 16 percent, and gave an agent's phone number. The returns seemed high to me, so I phoned and asked the agent if local taxes had inadvertently been included in the quoted return. She replied somewhat indignantly (and erroneously) that the tax did not apply to commercial real estate. She suggested that I talk with the seller, who operated a shop in one of the three premises.

In order to determine the basis of any negotiations, it pays to discover as much as you can about a property, the seller, and his motivation for selling. So off I went to his shop. There were no customers, so I introduced myself and asked him why he was selling the building. He replied very bluntly that he was far too busy to talk (remember he had no clients at that stage) and referred me to his real estate agent. While at the time it seemed frustrating that the agent did not know the answers to my questions, and the seller didn't make time to give me any answers, I also felt great about this situation. I knew that anyone else trying to find out anything about this building to help them determine whether they wanted to buy it would also face a dearth of information.

By talking with the remaining two tenants, I determined that the quoted returns of 16 percent were net of any taxes, and so I went back to the agent and suggested that I submit an offer. By now it was the middle of December, and her answer stunned me. "No," she said, "I cannot do that, as I am packing to go away on vacation."

"Wow!" I said, "must be some vacation. Where are you going? To Europe for six months?" She replied that she was only going down the road for a few days, but was adamant that she was too busy to be bothered with submitting an offer.

Once again, my reaction was "Great!" Every day that the owner could not muster the energy to talk about his building, and every day that the agent couldn't be bothered giving her client a written offer from a serious and interested buyer, the seller's expectation of purchase price had to be falling steadily.

In the end, she did not submit my offer until January 11, by which time I had reduced it substantially. It was not countered, but rather accepted "as is." Everyone was happy—the seller didn't have to answer any questions, the agent had her relaxed, uninterrupted vacation down the road without having to even think about submitting an offer, and I got a building for less than I had been willing to pay that December, and which in the years since has increased in value by a *factor* of five.

In the negotiation game, every bit of information is useful. Knowing that the seller and his agent were slow to respond, not focused, not on top of their game with facts and information, and a bit rude on top of it all, was useful. It meant that my competitors were more likely to be locked out of this game. I just sat back, lowered my offer, and ended up getting the property anyway, without even the hint of a competing buyer anywhere in sight.

All negotiations involve some give-and-take. I mentioned earlier a property that was advertised as being for sale at $12,000, but there was an error and the price should have read $120,000. The owner wanted to stay on as the tenant at $20,000 per annum. I decided to proceed with the acquisition, and had the property under contract at that price. However, just as I was about to close on the property, the seller announced unemotionally that in order for me to acquire the property, I now had to pay him $130,000.

My first reaction was, "You have got to be kidding! We have a contract at $120,000, so why on earth would I agree to pay you more?" He explained that if he only received $120,000, he could not pay off all his combined debt on the property, and so couldn't promise a clear title. I knew that I could pursue him for what is called *specific performance* (his failure to meet his contractual obligations), but I realized that with his debt loading, the chances of getting anything were pretty remote.

Instead of venting my dismay, I asked him why I should agree to paying $130,000. He replied that he would be happy to pay not just the agreed-upon rental of $20,000 per annum, but rather $22,000. The restaurant business could sustain this rental, so it seemed like a good solution.

Would you have agreed to pay him $10,000 more? Remember, the extra rental represented a 20 percent return on the $10,000. Think of your answer before reading on!

I did not pay him the extra $10,000. Instead, I said that I would *lend* him the extra $10,000, and that he would have to repay it on the earliest of (a) his default of the lease, (b) the expiry of the lease, or (c) the sale of his business. To cover myself, I took a chattel mortgage over his plant and equipment.

Five weeks after closing on the property, he sold his business, and I got my $10,000 back. In the meantime, of course, the rent was still $22,000 per annum. Thus my returns had increased from 16.67 percent ($20,000 of rental income divided by a purchase price of $120,000) to 16.92 percent ($22,000 of rental income divided by an initial capital outlay of $130,000) to 18.33 percent

($22,000 of rental income divided by the ultimate capital outlay of only $120,000). Also, the capital value of the property had increased on account of the greater rental income. I was better off in terms of cash flow, equity, and capital value.

The lesson is this: When situations arise that look like deal breakers, keep your cool and try to figure out a solution that will benefit everyone. I could have opted to sue the seller for specific performance. Not only would I have missed out on this deal, but I also would not have embarked on a joint venture with the seller (unlikely to have happened if we had ended up fighting over a lousy $10,000) in what turned out to be the most elegant restaurant, bar, and member's club in town. In fact, when Peter Jackson was directing *The Frighteners* (long before his fame as a director of the *Lord of the Rings* trilogy), the cast used to frequent our club, which is how I got to meet Michael J. Fox. In fact, my involvement in this property led to many lucrative real estate investments.

Other Negotiations

As a commercial real estate investor, your negotiation skills will be put to the test not only with real estate acquisitions, but you will also need to negotiate leases and their terms with prospective tenants.

When it comes to leases, avoid using the rental level as a negotiating chip. Try to establish the rental as being fixed and non-negotiable. Rather, negotiate on the number and location of parking spots allocated to the premises, the ability to use a storage room, your willingness to paint the interior of the premises prior to the tenant moving in, how many years you will grant them in their initial term, and how many rights of renewal you will give them.

Painting the interior of a large office may cost you as much as the rental income you would forgo dropping the rent for a tenant. However, the advantages of painting the interior over dropping the rent are threefold. First, you establish a base rental for the offices, which will come in useful when you are looking for tenants on other floors. You can cite this rental as part of the comps. Second, any future rent increases will be based on the higher rent and not on a discounted rent. And third, when it comes to appraisals, your building will appraise higher with the nondiscounted rents in place. This is because it is the rental income that is divided by the cap rate, and not the amount of money you spent painting (of course, a freshly painted interior will not have a detrimental effect on an appraisal).

Having just written that it is best not to drop the rent for any reason, I have nevertheless had situations where the tenants have asked for a reduced rental in the first year of a lease, in return for which they agree to spend money and effort making various improvements to the building. If the tenants are appropriately skilled, there is nothing wrong with this arrangement.

The wife of one of our tenants is an interior designer and offered her skills (and access to wholesale prices) to completely remodel the interior of her husband's offices. They did not ask for a reduction in rent. The office needed to be remodeled anyway, so we gratefully accepted the offer.

Overall, the trick to any negotiation is to think long-term. Most people think short-term. Well, in actual fact, most people do not think much at all, but when they do, they have a horizon that spans until the end of the week, and occasionally until the end of the month. Going back to the example of painting versus reducing the rent, on a short-term basis, reducing the rent is the more attractive offer. Painting requires a large injection of cash right now, whereas reducing the rent does not require a cash injection at all. However, when viewed long-term, painting is the better option. The cost is tax deductible, the building looks fresher, and, most important, your rentals remain high, so that the capital value stays high.

Before you enter into any negotiations, think about what your long-term outcomes are (rather than your short-term gains), and then structure a deal that has benefits for everyone. Be fair, be prepared to give a bit, and if the deal simply is not good enough for you, walk away.

CHAPTER 13

Financing Commercial Real Estate

While finding, analyzing, and negotiating great real estate deals may seem complex at first, the real art in acquiring commercial real estate is in arranging finance. As I keep saying, the deal of the decade comes along about once a week. Finding great deals is not a big challenge. If we had access to unlimited financing, we could acquire deal after deal. We need to learn how to get financing with confidence.

When I got started in real estate, applying for a mortgage was a formidable and nerve-racking task. This was in the days before independent loan originators, secondary market lenders, and ubiquitous lenders of last resort. If you wanted a mortgage, you applied for one at the bank.

You couldn't just walk in and ask for a mortgage. You had to make an appointment, and would be told to meet the manager at 2:15 P.M. on Tuesday in two weeks' time. You entered his office, where he sat in a huge oak chair behind a huge oak desk, while you were seated on a low camp chair on the other side of his desk. You felt as though you had to plead with the bank to condescend to even consider you for a loan.

How times have changed! The market has matured, and everyone has come to their senses to realize that money is a commodity. It's a bit like renting a car. If you land at a busy airport, it doesn't really matter which rental car company provides you with a car—they are all about the same quality, age, and price. If I need a car, and Hertz is out of stock, I don't throw a tantrum and complain, nor does Hertz admonish me for renting from a rival. All their cars are deployed, so they are happy, and my Avis/National/Europcar/Budget car works just as well.

A generation ago, banks demanded loyalty and generally got it. If you applied for a mortgage, the bank generally required you to switch all your accounts to this bank. I was applying for so many mortgages at so many banks that I found it easier to leave accounts open at all of them rather than to switch them all over every time I was forced to apply for a new mortgage at a new bank. I say "forced" because, after being successful with two or three mortgages at any one bank, they generally got wary of offering me more money, and I had to go elsewhere again. Now they have stopped this silly practice of forcing you to open new accounts, and they welcome new business with open arms and no strings attached.

In fact, banks are so keen to offer you mortgage finance, that they have roving mortgage managers who will now meet you at a time and place that suits you, including after work and on the weekends at your home. What a change from the days of having to set up an appointment with the bank manager at his office. Not only that, as the world gets increasingly connected online, it is becoming easier to apply for a commercial mortgage through the Internet.

While it may be easier to secure mortgage funding today than it was 30 years ago, it is still not a foregone conclusion that an application will result in a mortgage being advanced. The best you can do is maximize your chances of having your application approved. To achieve this, you need to understand the psychology of mortgage lenders.

Mortgage lenders and bank managers do not, in general, really understand real estate. If they did, they would quit their $90,000-a-year jobs and become investors themselves (as a few of my smart mortgage lenders have done, to my ease-of-funding detriment). Rather, they generally have an employee mentality, and their biggest fear is being fired, while their biggest aim is to get a raise at the end of the year.

How do mortgage lenders get a raise and avoid being fired? By having no bad debt on their books! Therefore, their primary concern when you walk in the door with your notes scribbled on the back of an envelope is not so much whether the property is a good deal for you, but whether the mortgage they are going to advance you is a good deal for them. Their worst fear is that your mortgage will fall over, not because you might lose your $30 million property, but because they might lose their 3 percent raise.

The best way to overcome this fear is to present them with overwhelming evidence that your property is so good that the chances of it falling over (and you defaulting on the mortgage) are so slim as to be negligible. The way I achieve this is through the proposal for finance.

Proposal for Finance

The aim of your proposal for finance is to convince your financier that the property you will use as collateral for the loan is indeed a great proposition. The worst thing you can do is lose his attention in a sea of numbers and facts, as his eyes will glaze over long before he has finished reading your lengthy treatise.

Therefore, on the cover of the proposal, put the words "Proposal for Finance," with the address of the property underneath; and below that, filling as much of the rest of the page as you can, put something that is worth a thousand words—a photo of the property.

A picture truly is worth a thousand words. Whether you are describing the friend you met in Brazil, the view from your mountain cabin in Bali, or the property you are trying to finance in Baltimore, a good picture will achieve in one second what a thousand words cannot achieve in an hour. That is why I offer photos in this book (albeit in black and white owing to production cost considerations) and why I post color versions of these photos and many others relevant to this book on my web site. These photos help you understand what I am talking about; satisfy any curiosity as to what these properties, parking systems, and other topics discussed look like; and generally give meaning to the words.

Given that photos can be so powerful, and that you are placing one on the front page of your proposal for finance, make sure it is a photo that puts the property in a good light. Take the photo on a sunny day (anything can look drab in the rain). Make sure there are no trash cans, piles of windblown litter, unsavory characters, stray animals, or faded "For Sale" signs in the picture, as any one of these can trigger your financier's fear about the property not being a good deal.

That's it! The first page is already finished. (See Figure 13.1.)

On the second page, place a simple table of contents to help the financier go to any particular section that he wants to review. The items to be listed here will become obvious as we proceed. See Figure 13.2 for a sample table of contents.

The third page will be the actual body of the proposal. I will cover two aspects here—the length of this section, and the psychological style in which it must be written.

As a teenager, I was lucky enough to learn Japanese. It was in the days before China had gained the prominence it has now, when Japan was quickly rising to become a dominant economic powerhouse. For a while I used to travel to Japan every eight weeks or so, and I became fascinated by the Japanese obsession with efficiency. Whether it was their houses, office layouts, transportation systems, or electronics, everything worked well and worked efficiently.

Fax machines had just been unleashed on the world (86 percent of which were manufactured in Japan) and, remembering that this was prior to the Internet, these machines for the first time allowed documents and pictures to be scanned and transmitted across the world. It was during this time that one of my business associates and mentors, Mitsutaka Kanai, impressed upon me the absolute power of a one-page document.

He pointed out that with a multipage document, no matter how meticulously you labeled the pages (for example, "page three of five"), and no matter how many paper clips or staples you used to keep the pages together (they would be removed for photocopying and faxing), the pages always risked getting separated and misplaced. Once separated from other pages, a proposal is

Proposal for Finance

1 Bay View Road, Cass Bay

Figure 13.1   **Front Page of the Proposal for Finance**

Proposal for Finance

Table of Contents

Summary
General Description of Property Offered as Collateral
Property Portfolio Statistics and Cash Flows
Statement of Assets and Liabilities

Appendixes:

Property Portfolio Statistics as of 14th September, 1992
Cash Flows, Property Portfolio, 1992–93
Statement of Assets and Liabilities
Consolidated Profit and Loss Account
Software Advertisement
Valuation Report, Cass Bay
Summary of Deed of Lease
Computer Analysis of Investment

Figure 13.2   **Table of Contents in Proposal for Finance**

Proposal for Finance

Summary: A mortgage of $95,000 is offered on a fully let commercial property, representing 73% of the acquisition price of $130,000 or 68% of the registered valuation of $140,000.   The rental of $22,000 p.a. represents a yield of 16.92%.

General description of property offered as collateral: The property is situated in Cass Bay, on the busy scenic drive between Lyttelton and Governors Bay, and constitutes the only commercial property in an exclusive residential settlement.   The tenant operates the prestigious licensed restaurant "Nordt's of Cass Bay," which is well known by locals and many Christchurch residents.   The property occupies the prime position in Cass Bay, with excellent access and visibility from the road, and panoramic views over the bay.

Nordt's of Cass Bay has been successfully run as a licensed restaurant by its present owner_____ for the past two years.   Prior to that, the restaurant was known as "The Three Crowned Herrings," and operated successfully on the same site for more than a decade.   Consequently there is a considerable element of goodwill that has been developed over the years.

A new Auckland District Law Society lease commences on 1st October 1992 for five years, with three renewals, each for further periods of five years.   Copies of the first two pages of the lease are included in the Appendix.

Property Portfolio Statistics and Cash Flows.   The property offered as collateral will form part of a portfolio with a total valuation (excluding the Cass Bay property) of $_____.   Complete details of the existing portfolio can be found in the Appendix. From this it is seen that the average *remaining* lease length is 5.42 years, while the debt-servicing ratio is a healthy 2.33.   Furthermore, the 1992–1993 budgeted cash flows are included in the Appendix, showing a pretax surplus of more than $_____ per year.

Statement of Assets and Liabilities.

Included in the Appendix is a Statement of Assets and Liabilities, showing total assets to be $_____ and total liabilities to be $_____, leaving a surplus of assets over liabilities of $_____ .

Figure 13.3   The One-Page Proposal for Finance

worthless. Conversely, there is zero chance of that happening with a single page document.

Furthermore, he said, with a single-page document, the reader can scan the entire contents without moving anything other than his eyes. Most importantly, a single-page document does not seem like an onerous task to wade through. It was the contention of Kanai-san that single-page documents actually got read immediately, whereas multipage documents were relegated to the "To be read" pile.

Consequently, I have always kept the body of my proposals for finance down to a single page, even on properties costing tens of millions of dollars.

Summary Paragraph

Singularly the most important paragraph in the proposal for finance will be the summary. This is where you let it be known just what you are proposing.

In the sample proposal in Figure 13.3 (regarding a property I ended up buying), the opening paragraph reads:

> *A mortgage of $95,000 is offered on a fully let commercial property, representing 73% of the acquisition price of $130,000, or 68% of the registered appraisal of $140,000. The rental of $22,000 p.a. represents a yield of 16.92%.*

Did I say "A mortgage is offered . . ."? Surely we are applying for a mortgage? Surely we want to say "A mortgage is requested" or "A mortgage is sought"?

We need to go on a small tangent here, as many investors,

even experienced ones, still do not know the difference between a mortgagee and a mortgagor.

Just as a lessor is someone who grants a lease (the landlord), and a lessee is someone who takes on a lease (the tenant), it is tempting to think that since we "apply to get a mortgage from the bank," the bank must be the mortgagor, and you must be the mortgagee. That is flat wrong!

To understand how this works, we need to remind ourselves of the transactions that take place when a bank funds your property.

Generally, when you want to buy a property, you don't have all the funds required to do so. Even if you do have the entire purchase price in cash, you agree it would be silly to pay cash for the property, as you would miss out on all the advantages of leverage.

Conversely, banks have the money required for the purchase but, fortunately, don't want to buy the property. I say "fortunately" because if they did want to buy it, they could, and you would miss out.

So you want the property but don't have the cash, and the bank has the cash but doesn't want the property. You go to the bank and essentially say, "If you give me the money I need to buy this property, I will give you a written pledge that I will faithfully pay interest every month, and in addition I will repay the principal."

In other words, the bank gives you the money, and you give them a written pledge. That pledge is called a mortgage, and that is why you, the investor, are the mortgagor, and the bank, as recipient of this pledge, is the mortgagee. You are giving the bank a mortgage in return for the cash.

This is why it is so important not to start your proposal for finance with the words "A mortgage is requested" or "A mortgage is desperately begged for" (bankers can smell desperation, and desperation often results in bad debt). In fact, you are not asking for anything! Rather, you are *offering* the bank something. Talk about turning the tables on your banker! Most clients want something from the bank ("Please may I borrow some money?"), and here you are making them an offer.

Most people feel awkward at best when asked to lend something to someone else. The words "May I borrow your digital SLR camera for my trip to Peru?" is not music to most people's ears. And yet those same people will be honored and curious if you offer them something instead ("Could I leave my Bugatti in your garage while I am on vacation in Peru so that the car can be driven once a week or so, to keep everything in great working condition while I am gone?"). What would you prefer—to be asked to lend your camera, or offered to drive your friend's Bugatti?

Applying for bank funding involves an exchange—money in return for a pledge. Why focus on requesting the money instead of on offering the pledge? Psychologically, when you ask for a mortgage, you are on the back foot, but when you *offer* a mortgage, things are different. Take note: In only six words ("A mortgage of $95,000 is offered") we have already gained an advantage.

Now the banker will want to know what is in it for him. How certain can he be that the interest will be paid? How much rental income is there to cover the mortgage? Well, let's review the opening paragraph:

> *A mortgage of $95,000 is offered on a fully let commercial property, representing 73% of the acquisition price of $130,000, or 68% of the registered appraisal of $140,000. The rental of $22,000 p.a. represents a yield of 16.92%.*

In this one paragraph comprising maybe three lines of normal text (it will depend on how many zeros are in the dollar amounts, among other things), you have managed to encapsulate the entire transaction. You want to buy a property for $130,000. It has an appraisal of $140,000. The rental income is $22,000 a year, giving a return of 16.92 percent. The property is fully leased, the LTV is 68 percent, and the loan-to-purchase-price ratio is 73 percent. Within the first 10 seconds of reading your proposal, the banker knows exactly why you are there and all the pertinent numbers of the transaction.

General Description of Property Offered as Collateral

This heading could simply be "General Description," but then a reader will be wondering "Of what?" You could simply put "General Description of Property," but you would miss out on a great opportunity to let the banker know that his investment with you is safe. By writing "General Description of Property Offered as Collateral," you are subtly reminding the banker that the very asset you are buying with the bank's funds will be used as security for those funds. You are offering him the property as collateral for the loan.

So not only are you offering him a mortgage, but now you are also offering him collateral for the loan. Through Cialdini's Law of Reciprocity,[1] at some stage, this banker is going to want to offer you something in return.

---

[1] Robert Cialdini, *Influence: The Psychology of Persuasion*, William Morrow & Company, 1984, 1993.

In this section, the text starts with, "The property is situated in Cass Bay, on the busy scenic drive between Lyttelton and Governor's Bay, and constitutes the only commercial property in an exclusive residential settlement."

Once again, you are using words to put the property in a good light. Could you simply have stated that "The property is situated in Cass Bay, on the road between Lyttelton and Governor's Bay . . ."? Of course you could have, but using the words "busy scenic drive" rather than merely "road" reveals that the road is busy, and likely to remain busy on account of its scenic quality, thereby attracting an ongoing stream of potential clients for the business.

In fact, can't you just write "busy scenic drive" even if the road is neither busy nor scenic? Think very carefully! It is my personal belief and philosophy that if you try to stretch the truth, even a little bit, you will eventually get caught out, and then everything you say will be put into severe doubt. Imagine if you wrote that the road was a busy scenic drive, and the banker happened to live around the corner and knew it to be neither, or he decided to take his family for a drive that weekend and discovered you had been exaggerating at best. He would probably dismiss everything else you wrote as an exaggeration as well. Perhaps the rental isn't even $22,000 per annum! Perhaps there isn't even a tenant! This guy stretches the truth!

Besides, would you really want to buy the property if the road (the channel through which your tenant will get all of his business) was not busy? For you to be interested in a property, it will have so many good features you can write about that you do not need to exaggerate or stretch the truth. Once your bankers know that you stick to the facts, it will make future mortgages even easier to arrange.

In this section, we effectively state that a new five-year commercial lease is in place, "with three renewals, each for further periods of five years. Copies of . . . the lease are included in the Appendix."

If you put a copy of the lease in the body of the proposal, the banker will never read it. In fact, the chances of him reading it in the Appendix are close to zero, but the fact that you have included it shows good faith and transparency—everything you claim in the summary can be verified. And all he really wants to know at this stage is (1) is there a good commercial lease in place, and (2) how long does the lease run?

Property Portfolio Statistics and Cash Flows

The property offered as collateral will form part of a portfolio with a total appraisal (excluding the Cass Bay property) of $_____. Complete details of the existing portfolio can be found in the Appendix. From this it is seen that the average remaining lease length is 5.42 years, while the debt-servicing ratio is a healthy 2.33. Furthermore, the 1992–1993 budgeted cash flows are included in the Appendix, showing a pretax surplus of more than $_____ per year.

Are you starting to see how powerful a short paragraph like this can be? We repeat the fact that the property is being offered as collateral. We show that there is already a healthy portfolio. (If this mortgage offer concerns your very first property, then rather than point out that the existing portfolio amounts to zero, just leave this section out, and talk about the budgeted cash flow for the subject property.)

The certainty of you being able to make mortgage payments is largely dependent on the length of your leases (and the quality of the tenants), which is why the banker will like to see what the average remaining lease length is on all your tenancies (these leases can be weighted for rental area, rental income, or a combination of both, to prevent the numbers from being unduly skewed by one or two aberrant leases).

Similarly, the debt-servicing ratio refers to the ratio of rental income collected to the mortgage payments that must be made. Collecting $2.33 in rent for every dollar of mortgage commitment puts a banker's mind at ease.

Finally in this section, tell the banker what the cash flow surplus will be. Again, do not put the spreadsheet here, as the banker will get bogged down in the detail, but summarize it in one sentence. You want to build confidence that this is a great investment, and that you are a wise and cautious investor.

Statement of Assets and Liabilities

All too frequently, people come up to me and ask defiantly, "What right does a banker have to know what my assets and liabilities are? I'll show him—I'll demand that he reveals his assets and liabilities to *me!*"

Well, he has every right. You are asking him to lend you money. In general, people don't like lending money, as nearly everyone has a bitter memory of lending money and never getting paid back. That is why I always chuckle at the conversation:

"Will you lend me fifty dollars?"

"Forty dollars? What do you want thirty dollars for?"

Well, banks and other lending institutions are willing to consider you for a loan. All they want is some reasonable assurance that you have the means and intent to repay the loan. The best way to determine your means and intent is to look at your track record, which is often best measured by your credit score and the scorecard of what you have achieved financially with your life so far—your statement of assets and liabilities.

Once again, a single sentence with a reference to the Appendix is most powerful. "Included in the Appendix is a Statement of Assets and Liabilities, showing total assets to be $1,200,000, and total liabilities to be $800,000, leaving a surplus of assets over liabilities of $400,000."

And there you have it—a one-page document that summarizes all the information that a banker wants to see in order to determine whether to lend you the money.

What to Include in the Appendix

How much information you include in the appendix will depend on the size and nature of the property. A forty-story office tower will require a much more elaborate appendix than a small restaurant in Cass Bay. For a small commercial premise on a standard lease, the page of the lease that spells out all the variables (lease duration, rent, etc.) may be sufficient. With larger properties, you will want to include copies of all the leases in their entirety.

Make the proposal for finance suit the property you are funding. If you are buying an $80 million office complex, then audited financials from a reputed accounting firm will be in order. If it is an $80,000 retail store, your own summary will probably suffice.

Absolutely include any lease documents, Assignments of Lease, variations of lease, and as many financial reports as you have or can generate within reason. Also, include more photos, so that the banker can get a good feel for the property.

Finally, as mentioned in Chapter 11, include a full printout of the reports generated by REAP. The banker may not agree with your assumptions, but at the very least he will agree that, based on your assumptions, you have a great deal under contract. More often than not, though, he will agree with your assumptions. Therefore, for your own selfish reasons, make sure you use reasonable assumptions so that you are not kidding yourself about how good the property is. Consequently he, too, will agree that it is a great deal, and your chances of getting the funds are almost assured.

Examples of full proposals for finance can be found on our web site, www.dolfderoos.com.

How to Use the Proposal for Finance

Great! So now you have your proposal for finance! Just what do you do with it? How do you use it?

The first thing I suggest is to print multiple copies. Be bold! Print 10 copies, or, if it is a large deal, 20 copies or more. Then visit each bank or financial institution in turn, and personally deliver the document, preferably to the person who is going to read it and decide whether to accept the mortgage. This lets the banker know that there is a real person behind the document and makes it more difficult to leave the proposal in the "To be read" pile. Also, let each bank know that you are approaching other banks. I often turn up not with just one copy of the proposal for finance, but 10 or 15 of them, and then I select one from the middle and say, "Here, this one is for you." This tactic has worked well for me. On one occasion, the banker involved looked at my pile of other proposals and said to me, "If I give you a commitment to fund this property right now, will you accept my offer?" He was scared that I would take the business elsewhere.

Like every other economic activity, supply and demand comes into play. If institutions are flush with funds, you can be bolder in trying to get a low interest rate, or playing one bank off against another. If funds are tight, you may need to be more willing to accept their terms. Either way, remember it is a game, and in 10 years' time it will no longer matter whether you initially financed a property through this bank or that insurance company. All that will matter is that you still own it, that rents have gone up and will continue to go up, and that the capital value also increases inexorably.

Once banks realize that you consistently produce quality proposals for finance that are not only accurate but always represent great deals, they will welcome your visits to their offices, taking the attitude, "What on earth has this wacky investor stumbled across this time?" They will relish being able to see how your statement of assets and liabilities has changed in the 10 months since your last visit. They will boast to their friends that they are your contact with the bank. They will ask you how you found this latest property, with just the slightest suggestion in their eyes that one day they, too, will give up their office cocoon and the security of a regular salary in return for the wild and exciting ride of being a maverick commercial real estate investor.

In fact, I always say that when you owe the bank $5,000, you have a problem, but when you owe the bank $5 million, *they* have a problem. And what happens when you owe the bank $5 million? They phone you a lot. Why would they phone you? To make sure you are still alive? To ask you if you are going to be able to make this month's mortgage payment? No, not at all.

Banks phone you when you owe them a lot of money, to invite you out to lunch. Now, you enjoy business lunches, and you are about to accept their kind invitation, when you remember that you went out to lunch with them the week prior, and they paid, so they probably want you to pay this time around. Before you can say anything, however, they say, "It's on us again."

Why, when you owe the bank millions, do they invite you out to lunch *and pay*?

The simple answer is that they want to give you more money. They would rather lend you another lump of $10 million or $50 million than lend it to complete strangers off the street, whose ability and willingness to pay they do not know yet. You have always paid the mortgage without fail and you have a great portfolio, so of course they want to lend you more money. They are now wooing you. The tables have turned completely, and it all started with the humble "Proposal for Finance" document.

One of the reasons I am so happy to use an example from way back in 1992 is that it shows that this format has stood the test of time. Sure, the words have been modified a bit over time and to suit local terminology, but in essence, what made it so powerful back then still applies. Unlike technology, the nature of real estate does not change much over time.

A big word of caution though, borne out of experience: If you are going to model your proposal for finance on the one here, do make sure you change the numbers to reflect the real estate you are looking to buy. I frequently get calls from bankers, especially after running an event, who through their laughter tell me that they have received proposals from a number of my students who copied my proposal without modifying the numbers.

Finally, while your initial proposal for finance may take the better part of a day to put together, once you have the first one done, any subsequent proposal for a different property will be relatively easy to create.

Umbrella Loans

With most properties you are looking at buying, you will probably apply for finance on each one individually. Bear in mind, however, that as your portfolio grows in size, you may reach a point where it is in your interest (and that of your major funder) to consolidate the portfolio and obtain an umbrella mortgage covering the entire cluster of properties. Usually these umbrella loans have a degree of flexibility such that new properties can be bought and added to the fold, or old ones sold and removed.

One big advantage for you is that it will reduce the application fees often associated with loan applications. Also, once you have built up sufficient rapport with a lender, they will accept another property into the mix essentially with just rudimentary checking on their part. This is helpful, not because you intend to pull the wool over their eyes, but because it cuts down on the time between application and approval.

CHAPTER 14

Structuring Commercial Real Estate Ownership

When starting out in real estate, it is tempting to want to put the ownership of your first acquisitions in your own name. Almost everyone I know started out this way. I, too, knew so little about the consequences of owning things personally that I also bought my first properties in my own name. However, of all the entities you can use to own real estate, owning it personally is just about the worst thing you can do.

Owning a property in your own name is unwise for financial reasons. Should you experience an unexpected financial crisis, then everything owned in your name is at risk—your home, your car, your iPod, your savings account—everything.

In most countries around the world, governments, to their credit, have sanctioned the use of entities that offer *limited liability*.

If one of these entities experiences an unexpected financial crisis, then the liability of the entity is limited to the assets of that same entity. The rationale for offering this liability protection is that many more people will be willing to establish businesses (and, in doing so, boost the economy) if they don't have to risk the shirt on their backs should the venture fail.

In the United States, the *limited liability company*, usually referred to by its acronym LLC, is one of the most common entities used to structure real estate ownership. An LLC is a flow-through device for taxation purposes, meaning that the net income (or loss) of an LLC flows through to the members (owners) of that LLC; the LLC does not itself pay tax.

In the United States, there are also C-corporations (C-corps) and S-corporations (S-corps), limited partnerships (LPs), limited liability limited partnerships (LLLPs), family trusts, and a host of other entities to choose from. To complicate matters further, the distinctions between them may be blurred—for instance, an LLC may elect to be taxed as an S-corp. Furthermore, you may want to consider investing through your individual retirement account (IRA), which may or may not be self-directed.

Other countries have their own mix of entities (with an entirely different set of names for them, not to mention rules). If you are investing abroad, you have to decide whether to use an entity from your home country or establish one in the destination country. Most big firms such as Microsoft, Sony, and Accenture have foreign subsidiaries. In general, if it is within the interests of a big multinational firm to set up a subsidiary in a foreign country, then there are probably compelling reasons for you to do the same.

Consequently, wherever you live in the world, choosing which entity is most suited to you can be a very complex issue. The most appropriate entity will depend on an intricate mixture of your age, marital status, number of dependents, financial circumstances, the state in which you reside, the state in which the income is derived, who manages the investments, and what you think you ultimately want to see happen with the net proceeds. It is entirely beyond the scope of this book to make suggestions or recommendations. More information can be found in some of my other books,[1] and there are publications, web sites, and structuring attorneys who focus on and specialize in this particular area. I recommend that, prior to closing on your first or next commercial real estate deal, you consult with a reputable attorney who can structure an entity that is best suited to you. A few weeks and a few thousand dollars spent doing this now can save you millions of dollars in the years to come.

---

[1]In particular, *The Insider's Guide to Making Money in Real Estate* (John Wiley & Sons, 2005); *Real Estate Investment and Management* (Success DNA, 2003); *The Insider's Guide to Real Estate Investing Loopholes* (John Wiley & Sons, 2005); and *The Insider's Guide to Tax-Free Real Estate Investments* (John Wiley & Sons, 2006).

CHAPTER 15

Managing Commercial Real Estate

As we saw in Chapter 3, the management overhead associated with commercial real estate is much less than that with residential real estate. Nonetheless, there are certain tips and techniques you can apply that will make your management experience much more pleasant.

You may opt to use the services of a property manager, in which case your only management concern is how to select the manager in the first place. However, you may also choose to manage your commercial real estate yourself, especially initially. One of the great benefits of doing this is that you will learn everything that is involved in commercial property management, thereby giving you a much better idea as to what to expect from property managers when you are ready to engage them.

Tenant Selection

The speed with which you can sign up a tenant applicant will depend on the supply and demand of tenants for your category of building in your area. If there is a chronic shortage of tenants, you may be more willing to sign up a tenant who, under different circumstances, you may not prefer.

The greater the likelihood of the rent being paid, the better. Thus, a property being leased by a country for its embassy should be a safer bet than the same property being leased by the Association of Retired Milliners. This is not to say that hat makers are unreliable, but their numbers are not exactly increasing noticeably, and their association may not be around for much longer. Similarly, an embassy compound leased to the government of Switzerland should be a better bet than the same compound leased to a little-known landlocked country that hasn't been around for long and is at war with its neighbor.

Government departments are the most solid of tenants, followed by large public companies and private companies. As the scale of the tenant gets smaller, you may request some supporting evidence to show that the company is creditworthy. At the small end of the scale, if a couple have set themselves up with a company to operate a retail store, you may want to ask for personal guarantees, so that if the business goes broke, the owners are still personally liable to pay the rent.

If prospective tenants will be moving from another location, drop by the old premises—how they keep them will be a good indication as to how they will keep yours.

Other than that, be willing to show prospective tenants your lease document, which spells out in great detail exactly what you expect from them. Remember, this is one of the advantages of commercial real estate: You are both dealing with contracts, not people.

Rule Enforcement

All the circumstances that would put a commercial tenant in breach of his lease are clearly spelled out in the lease, as are the remedial actions that you can take if such a breach occurs. However, the remedial action is not taken automatically. If a tenant fails to make his monthly rent payment, you must commence a series of actions to implement the remedies under the terms of the lease. For instance, you may have to send a letter pointing out the breach, along with your notification as to what action is being taken.

In this regard, the art of being a great manager is to be firm but fair, and friendly but not familiar. Take immediate action—that is being firm. Only take actions allowed for in the lease—that is being fair. There is no need to be nasty. One of the advantages of commercial real estate being so contract-centric is that you can enforce the rules and still be friendly. Finally, avoid being familiar. If you are too quick to have barbeques at each other's houses, babysit each other's kids, and wash each other's cars, you will inevitably have difficulty collecting the rent in times of economic difficulty for the tenant.

The great advantage of letting the word get out that you enforce the rules quickly and fairly is that tenants will realize they cannot get away with breaches for long. This way, when money is tight for them, they will seek out a slower-reacting creditor to not pay.

Rent Reviews

Rent reviews come around in accordance with the lease, typically every two or three years. You must have an efficient system of determining when a rent review is due on a lease, and then take steps to decide if it is appropriate to invoke an increase. You may determine this by observing what has happened nearby in terms of rentals, or by engaging the services of an appraiser who can make a rental appraisal or valuation.

Usually a lease will stipulate that a landlord's notice to increase the rent must be sent within a certain time frame, to give the tenant a chance to ponder and challenge the review. If he believes your suggested rent is not appropriate, he may engage his own appraiser, and if the two appraisals are far apart, then in accordance with the lease, an arbitrator may be engaged to arbitrate the matter. Again, everything is spelled out very clearly in the lease. The point to note is that you must have an efficient system of monitoring when all your rents are up for review.

How to Get a Tradesman to Do Your Work First

Finding a good tradesman is a bit like finding a good real estate agent or a good property manager. You have to be open to good referrals as well as seek new leads, interview many people, monitor those you choose to work with, and foster the relationship with those who stay in your fold.

As with any aspect of your life, clarity leads to power, so be very clear as to what the arrangement is between you and your tradesmen. I find that with any kind of relationship, the greatest source of disharmony is a mismatch of expectations. Thus, when it comes to dealings with your tradesmen and contractors, be very clear as to what happens when expectations are not met. For instance, who foots the bill of a cost overrun? Does anyone pay if a job takes twice as long as expected? Often, we will agree on a contract price, and then offer a bonus if the job is done sooner than the contract stipulates, and charge a penalty if the job takes longer. This is a great incentive for the contractors to quote accurate figures in the first place, and then to stick to these numbers (or better them).

Furthermore, I have a method of getting contractors to do my work first (before they do other clients' work), which is so spectacularly successful that I am stunned more people do not employ this tactic. I am all the more stunned, as I have been sharing this tactic at events for decades, and wrote about it in *Real Estate Riches* (John Wiley & Sons, 2004), and yet it would seem that the idea hasn't reached a tipping point.[1]

When you want a tradesman, you generally want him instantly (as your roof is leaking, or there is no electricity in a building, or a door won't lock). The antics other investors employ to get a tradesman to their property quickly always amuse me. They will try to lure them with the verbal promise of more work further down the track (this won't work, as the reason why they cannot come to your property quickly is precisely because they have so much other work going on). They will try to tempt them with the mention of an ice chest full of beer on-site.

My method is very simple and involves no bribery at all.

---

[1]Malcolm Gladwell, *The Tipping Point* (Back Bay, 2002).

Rather, I just rely on fulfilling expectations. I simply pay the tradesman or contractor the day the work is completed. None of this "I'll pay you on standard business terms at the end of the month," or "I'll pay you by the twentieth of the month following," as is common in some parts of the world, or "I'll pay you when I have completed my final inspection, and by the way, I am on vacation for six weeks."

If you happen to be on-site, perhaps inspecting the work, and they have fulfilled their side of the deal, pull out your checkbook there and then, and write out the check for the full amount. Most tradesmen will never have seen this before. Their jaw will drop, and they will go home and report that they have experienced something bizarre but pleasant.

If you are not on-site, see if your office can wire them the money directly into their account—it is faster and safer than posting a check. And if you have to resort to using an old-fashioned check, post it that very day. Your tradesmen will remember you for it, and the next time you have some work that needs doing, they will drop other work, knowing that once your job is done, the money is as good as in the bank.

Let's assume a contractor's bill comes to $20,000, and that you manage to delay payment for two months. Effectively, this delay will have saved you roughly 8 percent per annum over two months, or $267. However, since the interest on this opportunity cost would be tax deductible, the after-tax saving is really only about $150. Well, I am telling you that paying the $20,000 bill straight away makes my accounting much easier (no file with a bunch of bills with specific due dates), and the $150 that I otherwise would have saved buys me a lot of goodwill with my contractors.

Accounting

Speaking of accounting, commercial real estate tends to have very easy accounting requirements. You receive monthly rent payments by automatic bank transfers, pay the monthly mortgage payment by automatic bank transfer, and pay other bills such as insurance and property taxes by bank transfers. With just a few entries, the annual books are done. Usually, the tenants will pay the utilities directly, and often it is the tenants who even pay the insurance and property taxes directly. You may, of course, want to pay these items yourself and seek reimbursement from the tenants, on the basis that if they forget to make a payment, the insurance coverage or even ownership of the property could be in jeopardy. Either way, it will all be spelled out in the lease document.

Summary

The ease of managing a property will be in direct proportion to the clarity and quality of the lease document. In general, the larger, wealthier, and more prominent a tenant is, the fewer challenges you will have with the tenant, as their primary focus will be on moving their business juggernaut forward, rather than nit-picking with you over some minor aspect of the building.

Be firm, fair, and friendly, but not familiar. Pay all your bills the day you get them. Do not waste time fiddling with trivia on an existing property. Spend that time looking for your next acquisition.

CHAPTER 16

How to Beat the Average

In my book *Real Estate Riches*, I went to some length to explain how and why a real estate investment will, on average, beat a stock market investment. Furthermore, I presented my reasoning as to why it is difficult to beat the average in the stock market, whereas it is easy to beat the average in the real estate market. In this chapter I focus on why and how it is incredibly easy to beat the market average in commercial real estate.

First, statistics can be presented in many different lights to prove just about any point, as politicians well know. It is vital to understand the meaning and significance behind any set of numbers.[1]

---

[1] One of the best books to highlight this is Nassim Nicholas Taleb's *Fooled by Randomness: The Hidden Role of Chance in the Markets and in Life* (Texere Publishing, 2001).

I always get hoots of laughter and a few boos when I claim on stage, for instance, that "Here in Australia, half the population is of below-average intelligence, whereas in New Zealand, half the population is of above-average intelligence." Well of course half the population is of below-average intelligence in Australia, for the simple reason that the other half is of above-average intelligence. That's how the average comes about in the first place. If you were cynical, you could say that those doing the booing didn't understand the statement, and were from that half of the population that made the other half look good.

So let us be clear on what we mean by the *average*. The average is simply the numerical total of all the items you are considering, divided by the number of items. If the average age of citizens of a country is 36 years old, it simply means that when you add all the ages of the entire population, and divide that number by the total number of people, you end up with 36.

Consequently, when we consider the average capital growth of commercial real estate, we are talking about taking the percentage increase in capital value of every commercial property over a given time frame, and dividing it by the total number of commercial properties. In other words, the average takes into account every conceivable commercial property in the country.

Given this definition, there are many methods of beating the average.

Geography

The simplest and most predictable method of beating the average in commercial real estate is to invest in those geographic locations where growth rates are highest. Unlike most other markets (stocks, commodities, options, etc.), growth rates in commercial real estate tend to change very slowly over time, and tend to exhibit very minor fluctuations within a region. For instance, Phoenix, Arizona, is one of the fastest growing cities on this planet, and as a consequence, the growth in commercial real estate values has been sustained and steady. No investor has to sit behind a computer monitor, noting that, "Oops, today commercial growth is down—we'd better sell all our Phoenix buildings! Oh no, today everything is up, let's buy them all back!"

Capital growth of commercial properties was much higher last year in Arizona than it was in Wyoming. The same applied the year before, and the year before that. In fact, Arizona has outstripped Wyoming so consistently that it is a safe bet (if not a foregone conclusion) that Arizona will beat Wyoming again this year.

Because capital growth rates are relatively slow to change in any given region, it makes picking a location with predictably higher-than-average growth rates easy. Not only does Arizona have a higher-than-national-average growth rate, but there are parts of Arizona that consistently have a higher-than-state-average growth rate. For instance, Phoenix has a growth rate much higher than the state average. Similarly, within the greater Phoenix metropolis, there are towns that have a higher-than-metropolis-average growth rate, such as Scottsdale. And within Scottsdale, there are clusters of streets where there is a higher-than-Scottsdale-average growth rate, such as around Kierland or the Scottsdale Airpark. In other words, just by choosing a geographic location where for years, and sometimes even decades, capital growth rates have far outstripped the national average, you should be able to do better than average.

This ability to beat the national average on the basis of a judicious choice of geography is, of course, universal. In the United

Kingdom, the city of London has traditionally had growth rates much higher than the rest of the country. In New Zealand, Auckland and Queenstown for a long time now have outstripped average growth rates, and will probably continue to do so for a long time to come. In Australia, central Sydney, central Melbourne, and the Gold Coast have similarly exhibited growth rates far in excess of the national average. In South Africa, it is parts of Johannesburg and Cape Town that consistently outstrip the national average. This seems to me to be so obvious, that I am at a loss why more people do not choose to cash in on this legal handout.

One of the reasons why I enjoy the dynamics of the Phoenix market so much is because the growth is so mind-boggling. For instance, there is a section of downtown Phoenix bounded by Jefferson, Central Avenue, Roosevelt, and Seventh Street, which has over $3 billion in development going on at present. Arizona State University (ASU) has just opened its fourth campus there and expects 22,500 students and faculty within four years. They are opening the Walter Cronkite School of Journalism, a Nursing School, a 1-million-square-foot convention center, the headquarters for GenTech, and a slew of other big, bold buildings. As I write this, tracks are being laid for Phoenix's first light-rail system, a $7 billion project that will link Tempe with downtown Phoenix and other suburbs further west. In other words, the potential for capital growth in this region is huge, and puts the national average to shame.

You don't have to be in with the big boys, putting up a $300 million 40-story office tower to cash in on this tremendous growth. On the other side of Seventh Street, just shouting distance from all these construction projects, is an area known as the Garfield Historic District. It is full of smaller, older cottages that date back up to 100 years. Not too many years ago, this area was crime infested and dangerous, but over the past five years or so it has been undergoing a gradual but steady process of gentrification, where slowly but surely old houses are being done up and brought back to their former glory. The transformation is ongoing and startling.

However, I am not suggesting that you get involved with residential tenants. Read on . . .

Zone Changes

As downtown Phoenix is transformed into a vibrant area with new buildings, amenities, and countless people, the surrounding areas become popular for accommodation and a range of services that go hand in hand with such a dramatic increase in population. Inevitably, pressure is put on the city council to allow for some zone changes from residential to commercial, and this suddenly opens up a whole new market to commercial real estate investors.

For instance, with a group of investors, we have taken some positions on houses in the Garfield district that have either been granted a zone change or are undergoing one, which will enable commercial uses such as professional offices, art galleries, wine bars, or coffee shops (remember, I am also still looking for premises for two hairdressers). With a proximity to the bustling growth district of downtown Phoenix, and a pending zone change that should allow for rentals far greater than you would ever get from residential tenants, these properties are set to increase in value by an incredibly wide margin over the national average.

Proximity to Views

Commercial buildings with great views will always command premium rentals over those with inferior views. Office towers overlooking lakes, rivers, or valleys, or with views of mountains, will continue to rise in value faster than average. Consequently, properties with great views will beat the average easily.

Remember our discussion on air rights. Be willing to pay for air rights to have your property retain views that would otherwise be lost. Conversely, be willing to charge air rights for a neighbor to retain his views.

The Center of Town

Another strategy that consistently beats the average is to invest in the hearts of the downtown areas of many cities. Attorneys, dentists, doctors, and accountants may opt to leave the center of a city to relocate their offices in the suburbs, where parking is cheaper and easier and where it is easier for their clients to access them. However, there will always be core activities that are well suited to being in the center of town. These activities and businesses include consulates and embassies, airline headquarters, television stations, and the headquarters (regional or national) of prominent law firms and accounting offices.

Furthermore, while suburbs tend to sprawl in all directions, real estate in the centers of cities remains in short supply, and therefore capital values tend to rise faster than average.

High Technology

Buildings that have a lot of high technology incorporated in them may appeal to a smaller set of potential tenants, but in general, these tenants are willing to pay a premium for these facilities. Also, the tenants generally stay longer for the simple reason that it will be difficult to find the same set of technology features elsewhere.

At present I am involved with the creation of what will be the largest private medical facility in New Zealand, at Albany, north of Auckland. (See Figure 16.1.) The buildings and facilities will be

Figure 16.1   **High-Tech Health Park in Albany, Auckland, New Zealand**

so specialized that they will not really be suitable for any other purpose than that of a medical complex. By the same token, rental growth should be high, and tenant turnover extremely low.

A high capital growth may be reflected in a low cap rate, but a low cap rate does not take the growth out of capital growth!

Leasing and Management Tactics to Beat the Average

Apart from choosing the right location to beat the average, there are all manner of tactics and techniques you can apply to beat the average returns. Many have been discussed in earlier chapters, such as how you can attract a tenant while other landlords cannot, or how to manage a property firmly and effectively.

Combining All Methods of Beating the Average

I have presented some tactics you can use to beat the average capital growth on commercial real estate. These tactics need not be used in isolation. For instance, if you buy a building in Phoenix, Arizona (which already has a growth rate much higher than the national average), on a street where a zone change is about to go through, and this building is close to the downtown area that is experiencing higher-than-average-Phoenix growth, has tremendous views, and is decked out in the latest of high-technology access and communications facilities, then you can live in confidence that your investment will far outstrip the average capital growth rate for commercial property by a wide margin!

The chance of being able to combine all these tactics may be small, but be open to the possibility of combining two or three of them. Once you develop this kind of nose for ferreting out excellent properties, you will be surprised how regularly you can find them.

What it all boils down to is that the best way to beat the average is to think differently. Average thinking leads to average results. Extraordinary thinking leads to extraordinary results. Or, to put it another way, the average person does not think. Remember, half the population is of below-average intelligence! Think, and you can easily beat the average.

CHAPTER 17

Raw Land

In my world, buying commercial real estate means that there are buildings in place in which commerce is already being conducted the day you buy the property. I have always been an advocate of buying existing buildings, for the simple reason that I have always wanted rental income from day one. When I was starting out, this requirement was born out of necessity: I was not in a position to buy a property unless I could justify the loan using the rental income. Even today, I prefer the certainty of regular, monthly income that a building provides, over the speculative expectations of increases in the value of raw land.

There are only three reasons to consider buying raw land. The first is to use the land for farming. From my experience of talking with many farmers, farming is not a lucrative business. I know farmers who work seven days a week, sometimes for 10 or more hours a day, and when all is said and done, they earn maybe

$120,000 a year. This may sound like a lot of money, but first of all, the hourly rate is lousy, and second, the net income is pathetic when you consider that their farm may be worth $4 million. Even if they didn't have to work 70 hours per week, the income of $120,000 would only represent a lousy 3 percent return on investment (ROI). They could sell the farm, invest the $4 million, easily earn 10 percent or $400,000 a year, and have all the time in the world to read books, travel the world, and visit with friends.

Despite this logic, most farmers do not sell their farms. For many, they simply work so hard that they do not have time to sit down and realize the folly of their daily grind in the face of the far more lucrative alternative of selling and investing the proceeds. Others are willing to suffer the low returns in order to be able to live their beloved farm lifestyle. For some, their farm has been in the family for generations, and they don't want to be the ones to "sell the family silver," so the family is condemned to long hours and low returns for yet another generation.

There are, of course, exceptions to low farming returns, as we will see shortly and in Chapter 18.

The second reason to consider buying raw land is to develop it. Every real estate investor comes face-to-face with the temptation to buy some land, construct some buildings, do some landscaping, and sell the entire project for hundreds of times what the development will have cost. Developing is so tempting because on paper the profits are so incredible. Not only are the profits great on paper, but they can be incredible in reality as well—so much so, that when a developer has completed one project, he is compelled to embark on another one that, for reasons of ego, has to be larger than the one prior. In this manner, the developer makes more and more money completing bigger and bigger projects. This would all have a happy ending except for one thing: an unexpected economic downturn.

It is almost inevitable that developers get caught out in a downturn. It is not just that interest rates may go up a bit, or that demand for the product they are creating declines a bit. Rather, it is a combination of all these things. A glut of product on the market (as other developers are also hurting, and therefore offering their stock at cutthroat prices), difficulties in securing mortgage funding, increased interest rates, declining demand, a general fear of investing in real estate, contractors taking twice as long to complete a task as quoted, and expenses going way above budget—all of a sudden these factors conspire to cause a developer to go belly-up. I have seen it happen through multiple economic cycles in many countries. Developers make increasingly large profits and take on increasingly large projects, until all of a sudden they go under. (Meanwhile, whatever interest rates, demand for new stock, or contractor rates are doing, the humble though not nearly as flamboyant commercial property investor just sits there taking in rent from his collection of commercial buildings month after month. Over time, the rents increase, and therefore so do the values of his buildings. And he does all of this without nearly as much effort as the developer.)

The third reason to buy raw land is in anticipation that it will go up in value. This, of course, is pure speculation, which is a slightly more respectable word for gambling. One of the challenges with land speculation is that since there is no income generated during the period of ownership, banks in general will not lend money to buy land. Furthermore, even if they did, the mortgage interest is not tax deductible, as you can only claim those expenses incurred in generating taxable income, and there is no income generated from the land. You could claim that speculating in land is your business, but then you would not get a low capital gains tax rate on the profits, as you have already admitted that the commodity you trade in is land—it is your trading stock.

Nevertheless, like many real estate investors, it was perhaps inevitable that I get involved in raw land deals.

Best Choice Properties

In August 1999, I went to Bali, Indonesia, to make a presentation to a private U.S.-based company. There were many people present, all of whom had spent large sums of money to be there, but two of them, Ross Denny and Randy Carder, stood out from the crowd as being determined *and* lateral thinkers, a rare combination these days.

The next time I met Ross and Randy was the following year in Cairo, Egypt, when I spoke at an event at the Oberoi Hotel, literally a stone's throw from the great pyramids. We got to know each other a bit more, stayed in touch, and three years later found ourselves all living in Phoenix, Arizona. We joined forces to run the Best Choice Group of Companies.

From 2002 to 2005, the greater Phoenix area was experiencing unprecedented growth in capital values of just about every category of real estate imaginable. While Phoenix had enjoyed solid and above-average growth rates for the previous 50 years, in this period the growth seemed to take off as if propelled by a guided missile headed for the stratosphere.

For readers unfamiliar with the Phoenix area, let me give some background as to why the region was and continues to be so popular. The climate in Phoenix is spectacular and very easy to get used to. Apart from 10 or so weeks during the height of summer, when temperatures can stay above 100°F (around 40°C) for a few weeks on end, the weather is just perfect, with 350 sunny days a year and low humidity. The job market is stable and growing, with many high-tech firms having headquarters or major centers here, such as Motorola, IBM, Honeywell, and Rockwell. Google has just relocated from Silicon Valley to Phoenix. There are many call centers such as the one for US Airways, and a plethora of other employers.

For a long time now, some 6,000 people have been moving into the greater Phoenix area every month. This provides ongoing demand for anything from podiatrists, hairstylists, and coffee shops to all flavors of real estate.

For a number of years, we were actively engaged in a wide variety of real estate ventures. We had bought orange groves, subdivided them into residential developments, and even had some of the homes constructed. We were involved with commercial retail development in outlying suburbs. However, like anyone operating in this fast-growing market, we couldn't fail to see what was happening with land prices.

We had seen speculators buy land for a few hundred dollars an acre, only to sell it a few months later for twice as much, or even five times as much. You can only observe that for a limited time before you develop the desire to give it a go yourself.

We knew that being successful with land development or speculation required more than just buying some dirt, sitting on it, and selling it at a profit. Despite the tremendous growth in the region, there were vast tracts of land that were not part of the general upsurge in values. So we pooled our collective knowledge, researched areas, studied population trends, met with companies that specialize in monitoring real estate trends, and looked at a lot of pieces of land. After conducting this research for what seemed like years, we were ready to make some moves.

On one deal, we contracted to buy 1,120 acres of land near Tonopah for $760 an acre. We had plans to develop this land, but barely five months after acquiring the property we received an offer of $2,500 an acre. We had to make a decision: Accept the offer for a great profit, or continue with our original plans, hoping to make even more. That week I was lecturing on an investors' cruise in the Caribbean, and managed to get in telephone contact with Ross and Randy when the boat stopped in Puerto Rico. I spent a good chunk of that evening on the phone with them while I wandered the streets of San Juan, debating the relative merits of selling versus holding. The three of us were definitely not in agreement as to what to do, but we run the company democratically, and, by a vote of two to one, we accepted the offer.

Not one year later, the property sold again, this time for $9,000 an acre. Tough as this news was to stomach, we rationalized that the profits we took out were deployed into other deals that we could never have made had we not taken our profits on this deal. In general, Best Choice uses equity funding rather than debt funding. The sale of our land enabled us to grow the company internally rather than seeking further growth capital externally (which comes at a price, like most things). And, in deference to my constant reminders of the need to create long-term passive income, we carved off 20 acres of the original 1,120 to develop into commercial space, which we still own.

Carving off the 20 acres also highlights another aspect of our strategy. As I detail elsewhere in this book, most developers sell their entire inventory at the completion of each development, choosing to plow their profits into their next, bigger deal. This is fine so long as the market stays strong, but eventually the market turns, and inevitably some developers get caught and go under. Had they retained a portion of their developments on a long-term hold basis, they would have been in a much stronger position during any downturn.

While this 1,120-acre land transaction can be categorized as pure speculation, we also became developers all over town. We employed people and paid for them to become general contractors, so that they could supervise the construction of our own projects. We aggregated houses, got a zone change, tore the houses down, and embarked on putting up commercial buildings.

We were doing so much landscaping on our own properties that we set up Best Choice Landscaping, which at its peak employed 18 people and had fleets of Bobcats, water tankers, trucks, and bulldozers. It was so successful that we took on contracts for outside work as well, including the contract to look after the landscaping for the Mayo Clinic facilities in the valley.

Our in-house consumption of trees, bushes, and shrubs for landscaping was so great (8,000 on one project alone) that we turned some of our land into a nursery. Given that we had a very reliable and creditworthy client (ourselves) who guaranteed to buy our entire crop, the returns on our tree farm were set to be very healthy, and not at all in the 3 percent category of most farmers, lamented earlier.

And, as if growing tens of thousands of trees wasn't an odd enough activity for otherwise hard-core real estate investors to be involved in, we considered setting up a fish farm for another real estate project that required 35,000 fish. . . . Let me explain.

Spring Mountain Ski Ranch

Most people are surprised to learn that although Arizona is a landlocked state, the number of boats per capita is greater than in either California or Florida. People in Arizona are boat-crazy, and consequently the line to put your boat in the water at nearby Lake Saguaro on a typical Saturday morning is over three hours long.

About 10 years ago, a group of 10 water-ski fanatics got together and agreed to create a water-ski facility on 168 acres of land about an hour from downtown Phoenix. Their company had an operating agreement that was no doubt drafted with good intent. In order to discourage the water-ski fanatics from falling out with each other, the agreement stated that if ever they should disagree, they would sell the entire project at the original cost price.

For four and a half years, these water-skiers worked on their zone approvals, applications for water rights, and the myriad of other legal hoops that must be negotiated in order to construct something as significant as 48 acres of lake. They almost got everything completed, and then must have had the falling out that the clause in the operating agreement so valiantly tried to avoid. Well, this clause ended up being invoked. For us and our partners, it was a matter of being at the right place at the right time, and we picked up the project complete with all approvals and pending applications, for a price that had been fair years earlier. (See Figures 17.1 through 17.3.)

Now, some three years on, two of the four lakes are in place. Phase one of our two-phase development has been completely sold out, and we are waiting on what is oddly called a "bathing permit" to enable us to dig the two remaining lakes.

The need for the fish should now be apparent. Artificial lakes are prone to algae blooms and can harbor the larvae of many kinds of bugs. Specific species of fish are needed that don't eat each other, but can remove all the unwanted aquatic plants and insects that would otherwise grow and breed prolifically. However, for reasons explained in the next section, we decided not to breed our

Figure 17.1   **Fleets of Earthmoving Machinery Preparing to Dig Our Lakes**

Figure 17.2   **Aerial View of Water-Ski Lakes Being Developed**

Figure 17.3   **Spring Mountain Ski Ranch**

own fish, and opted instead to have them trucked in, thousands at a time.

The Benefit of Having Great Partners

Great partners are, of course, beneficial to any venture. As it turns out, Randy, who was raised in Washington state, grew up around water-skiing. It ended up becoming a passion. Randy became a certified water-ski instructor, had his own water-ski school, and skied some of the certified tournaments around the country. Clearly, his background, even if serendipitous to our project, turned out to be extremely advantageous for us in developing Spring Mountain Ski Ranch. First, he knows about things that the rest of us hadn't even conceived, such as the need to create lakes with specific slopes so as to reduce the wake from boats and skiers as soon as possible after they have passed. Second, his contacts in the industry have been immensely useful, not only during the construction phase, but also with respect to the selling of lots and the running of the entire operation.

A passion that Randy and Ross share is car racing. While Randy races dirt late models, Ross races remote-controlled scale models. It is not an idle hobby. Currently, Ross is the Arizona state champion, and he also won the 2007 United States Gas Championships. Not only does this take Ross all over the country for race meetings, but Ross has created what is now touted by the industry as the nation's best racetrack outside Phoenix. Even with our hobbies, we cannot separate real estate from our thinking!

More recently, with Curt Denny joining the team as a fourth partner, we have covered many of the basic skills needed for our operation. If all partners had the same set of skills, then arguably some people would be redundant. Rather, our skills are complementary, with some of us focusing on business structuring and compliance, project management, liaison with contractors, communications, equity funding, customer relations, and reporting, in addition to the core activities of sourcing, analyzing, negotiating, and acquiring pieces of real estate.

In fact, it was Curt's search for a home to live in that led us to what could turn out to be our biggest project yet, involving 12 acres in the heart of Hollywood. This project is commercially sensitive and will have to be written about in a subsequent publication.

The point is that if you can assemble of group of people who may have wildly varying backgrounds, ages, interests, religions, circumstances, and points of view, but who nonetheless share a passion for excellence, a desire to do good, the drive to get the job done no matter what, and a genuine zeal for real estate, then you have the makings of a formidable force in real estate.

Getting Back to Commercial Real Estate Investing

While our forays into landscaping, tree growing, and general contracting were educational and largely fun, we are no longer involved in those activities. For instance, despite all the advantages of our own group of companies having an in-house landscaping company, the forward planning and logistics required to keep 18 men and a fleet of machinery efficiently deployed on a wide range of projects is enormous. Randy would be on-site at 5 A.M. and not get home until late. His focus on keeping that team usefully deployed prevented him from doing more interesting—and ultimately more lucrative—things elsewhere.

In a wise move, like so many people from all walks of life before us, we decided to divest ourselves of all noncore activities, and focus again on what we know best: smart real estate deals where we have identified a twist that we can capitalize on to vastly increase value. Best Choice Properties continues to work with equity partners from all over the world to create value with real estate transactions that are, in general, a lot of fun.

CHAPTER 18

Extraordinarily Odd Commercial Deals

John Baen is the most enthusiastic real estate investor I have ever come across. Born in California but bred and raised in Texas, he has a quick patter, an infectious and hearty laugh, and a passion for real estate that is second to none. He is a licensed agent, broker, and appraiser, and is often called upon by the courts to be an expert witness in disputes involving real estate. For decades, John Baen has been a professor of real estate at the University of North Texas (UNT), where he is adored by students. Every year he holds an alumni gathering on his huge ranch an hour west of Denton, and students from the past decades come from all over the world to catch up with each other and exchange real estate stories.

I first met Baen, as he prefers to be called (not Professor Baen, not Dr. Baen, not even John Baen, just Baen) when he was appointed the first chair of the new Department of Property and Valuation Studies at Lincoln University outside Christchurch, New Zealand, where I was living at the time. We would both be speaking at the national conference of Harcourts Real Estate (or some other real estate firm), or meet at other real estate–related events. I clearly remember his flamboyant style and the power of his message.

After two years at Lincoln, Baen returned to UNT in Texas. Soon thereafter I, too, was in Texas, involved in a bid to acquire the Republic Tower in downtown Dallas, a complex comprising three towers of 50 floors, 30 floors, and 8 floors respectively, with 1.92 million square feet of leasable space, which was for sale at way below the replacement cost of $400 million. The building had a number of serious issues, and we ended up bidding $15 million. Our bid ultimately was unsuccessful, but the winning bid was a mere $25 million.[1]

A couple of years later, I moved to San Francisco and traveled to Texas regularly, working on various deals, such as the Bank One Tower in Fort Worth mentioned earlier. Baen was always willing to offer advice and help out in any way he could. We ended up running a weekend event together. We partnered on a couple of deals. A year or so later, I was appointed visiting professor at UNT. I got to know Baen a little better each time.

And suddenly it dawned on me: Despite Baen's obvious and broad knowledge on all kinds of real estate, he had a passion for oil deals.

---

[1]I have discussed this property in greater detail in my book *Real Estate Riches*.

Oil in Them Thar Hills

In most countries, if you strike oil or minerals on land you own, you do not automatically own the oil or minerals. Most governments have decided that a citizen may own the title to a piece of land, but the government owns anything of value underneath it.

One of the great things about the United States is that the owner of a piece of land owns whatever is underneath it. Thus, if you strike oil in your backyard, it is yours to sell, lease, borrow, or develop. Conversely, if you sell the land, then the new owner has the rights to any minerals.

In fact, only in the United States do private investors own a patch of property all the way to the center of the earth and into the sky. In this sense, real estate truly is the basis of all wealth. It includes everything on the land (buildings and structures), over the land (air rights), and under the land (minerals, oil, gas, water, thermal energy, etc.).

In Texas and Oklahoma, things get even better. In these two states, the ownership of the land and the ownership of the minerals can be separated. In other words, you can buy a piece of land, split off the minerals, sell the land without the minerals, and then go about mining the minerals, even though you no longer own the land. And in Texas, mineral rights are perpetual. These rights are the icing on the cake.

Baen has shaped mineral rights into an art form, and the icing on the cake (the mineral potential) has become the cake. The cost of drilling an exploratory well to see if there is any oil or gas can be enormous—millions of dollars. However, oil companies are willing to do this free of charge to you and give you a small percentage (12 to 25 percent royalty) of the output of the well should it be productive, in return for you giving them the contract to drill on your mineral rights, even if it is no longer your land. (See Figures 18.1 through 18.3.)

Baen sits on many oil and mineral rights all over Texas. Some still need to be drilled to see if the wells will be productive. Some have been drilled and turned out to be dry (although new technology introduced by oil companies in the past five years ensures that some 90 percent of wells drilled these days are productive). And others are quietly producing oil or gas with no overheads to Baen—no leaking roofs, tenant complaints, or other challenges associated with conventional commercial real estate investment.

I, too, have become an oil man, and while my income from this operation may not be spectacular, I get a certain satisfaction

Figure 18.1   **John Baen with Dolf in Texas, 2003, Getting Ready to Drill a New Well**

Figure 18.2   Lunch Break with the Oil Drilling Team

Figure 18.3   John Baen with Dolf at Another
Texas Oil Rig, Drilling for Oil

knowing that my share of oil that is pumped out of the ground is far greater than the oil I consume in vehicles.

Marine Farms

If oil deals where you do not even own the land seem odd from a real estate perspective, then even odder are my marine farms in the Marlborough Sounds in New Zealand. With the entire operation being out at sea, it stretches the meaning of the word *real* in real estate.

The Marlborough Sounds are an extensive waterway in the northern part of the South Island of New Zealand. The fractal shores in fact comprise one-fifth of the length of New Zealand's coastline. With unpolluted waters, an abundance of nutrients, and shelter from the open sea, these sounds provide the perfect environment for shellfish to grow. (See Figure 18.4.)

Figure 18.4   **Marlborough Sounds, with One-Fifth of the Length of New Zealand's Coastline**

The waterways are highly regulated. Limited numbers of licenses are granted, as overharvesting would be detrimental to the entire industry. Consequently, licenses have considerable value even before a crop is harvested.

My farms grow oysters and mussels. The *spat* is seeded on lines that hang vertically in the water from floating racks. Depending on water temperature, nutrients, and a number of other factors, the shellfish may be harvested anytime from around 7 months to 18 months. Once harvested, the crops are sold on the open market either for local consumption or, more typically, to be airfreighted to Asia or America. As such, prices are global, being affected by world supply and exchange rates.

Always be willing to expand your concept of commercial real estate to include anything where commerce is conducted within geographically defined spaces, be it on land, in the air, at sea, or, dare I say it, out in space.

CHAPTER 19

Property Ventures Limited

Back in the 1990s, I was approached by a number of people (mostly readers of my early books) and asked to put together a syndicate, so that they could participate in some of my deals. I was somewhat wary of having partners, as I had seen that the greater the number of people involved in a deal, the greater the chances of there being a major disagreement and things spinning out of control. I decided to see what interest there would be in a syndicate of some kind, on the basis that if there was little or no interest, I could put the idea to rest once and for all.

To run my test, I contacted Dave Henderson. I had come across Dave on a number of occasions over the years. He has more drive and energy for business in general, and real estate in particular, than anyone I know. He was involved in setting up the Ripley's Believe It or Not museum on the Gold Coast of Australia, putting in car racing tracks, and creating an international ice cream company, amongst his many ventures. On top of all that, he was also an active real estate punter.

Dave is also incredibly well read, and is a staunch libertarian. Not happy to just share his views on libertarianism with acquaintances, Dave spent his own money to set up a national radio network called Radio Liberty, which took the country by storm. Every Saturday, I would fly to the capital, Wellington, to host the two-hour *Real Estate Show*, which, in a country already crazy about owning property, was a hit.

Dave and I crafted a questionnaire to mail to my database of then 3,000 people. (How things have changed in the past dozen or so years—these days a survey is done over the Internet, and our database now has well over 160,000 investors.) To discourage anyone but the most serious investors, we had five pages of questions that would take some considerable effort to complete. To our amazement, from the 3,000 questionnaires we sent out, we got over 700 replies. One thing was very clear: You cannot undertake a syndicate with 700 people. We had to go back to the drawing board.

After many deliberations about the relative merits of setting up a public company, we enlisted the services of a lawyer and an accountant, and set out to create a prospectus.

Getting a prospectus approved by the relevant authorities in any country is a time-consuming and often disheartening task, especially for a company with no capital to start off with, and no project to identify as the initial deal. It took more than a year to get the prospectus approved, and we then set about printing it.

Most prospectuses are printed as high-quality booklets, with translucent pages revealing beautiful photos of the project being undertaken. A print run can cost hundreds of thousands of dollars, an expense that ultimately, of course, the investors lured in by the glossy prospectus end up paying for.

Consequently, our prospectus was photocopied onto white paper. When we sent it out to potential investors, the cover letter read, in part, "This is probably the cheapest looking prospectus you have ever seen. It is fully intended to be so, as the sole purpose of this company is to make money for its shareholders."

At the time, a lot of public real estate investment companies were being criticized for some of the excesses of their directors. One well-known company, for instance, had just posted a loss, and yet the directors granted themselves a combined salary increase of $800,000. When, at the annual general meeting, shareholders asked why they would give themselves such an obscene increase in the face of a loss during the year and no dividends, the directors simply replied, "Because we can."

Consequently, our prospectus made one thing very clear: There were to be no overheads whatsoever paid for by the company—no salaries, company cars, offices, corporate planes, secretaries, or expense accounts. All officers' rewards were to be performance-based. I think that this strategy struck a chord with the investing public.

The total funds collected amounted to some NZ$1.8 million, not a lot in the scheme of such things. At one stage we even debated whether we had sufficient capital to have a good chance of making this company fly. However, we decided to proceed, and made our first purchase for $2.3 million, offering script in the company as part of the purchase price.

This first acquisition was a block of farmland, situated in the beautiful Gibbston Valley close to Queenstown, New Zealand. By getting local council approval for a change of use, and turning the land into vineyards, and of course with the relentless passage of time, the value of this property has increased tenfold. (See Figures 19.1 and 19.2.) Still on the drawing board for this project is a boutique hotel and spa resort with a grape theme.

Another early acquisition was a derelict building that had been used as a woolen mills factory. This was acquired for $1.7 million and, after spending some $4.6 million to convert it to upmarket student accommodation, was appraised at over $12 million. There was such a demand for quality student accommodation that the company went on to convert or build other facilities all over the country, making us the largest providers of student accommodation in the nation.

Figure 19.1   **Our Vineyards in the Beautiful Gibbston Valley**

Figure 19.2   **From Sheep Station to Vineyard in Four Years**

This building was our first acquisition in Christchurch. The building next door was used as a massage parlor, and one day it burned down, probably as a result of ongoing rivalries between competing massage parlor operators. Anyway, we bought the land and have converted it into His Lordship's Lane. Minx Restaurant, which looks out over this lane, now attracts the highest rentals per square meter of any restaurant in Christchurch, at over $300/m².

Over time and under the energetic and determined stewardship of Dave Henderson, the company has come to own or control some 85 acres of downtown Christchurch. The company has created upscale restaurants, coffee shops, wine bars, open piazzas, walking lanes, retail space, offices, and residential accommodation. It is entirely fair to say that what the company has undertaken in Christchurch has completely changed the heart and pulse of the city.

Property Ventures Limited has also completed a number of major land subdivisions overlooking beautiful lakes in the South Island of New Zealand. It has developed its own hotel brand, Hotel So, which offers a new concept in high-tech inner-city accommodation at a very affordable price. There is also LivingSpace, the division that provides upmarket student accommodation. The biggest project of all, however, is Five Mile.

Five Mile

What started as a dream is now starting to become a reality. Framed by dramatic mountain ranges, Five Mile is situated on over 80 acres of flat greenfield land near the beautiful town of Queenstown, which is known as the outdoor adventure capital of the world. The site commands exceptional views of some of the area's foremost geographical features, including the Remarkables, Lake Wakatipu, Cecil Peak, and Peninsula Hill. (See Figure 19.3.)

Five Mile is a significant new town concept. We have master-planned a development that will include a wide range of real estate, from residential apartments, live work units, commercial office space, and LivingSpace accommodation, to numerous retail tenancies, a university campus, light industrial buildings, civic buildings, and a significant amount of public open space.

Five Mile was planned by world-renowned Florida-based urban planners Duany Plater-Zyberk, and will set a new standard in New Zealand in all areas of development. Five Mile is, at $2.2 billion, the largest single project that Property Ventures has undertaken to date and is likely to take over 10 years to complete.

Figure 19.3   Aerial View of Five Mile, New Zealand

This section is by no means meant to be a definitive treatise on the history and phenomenal growth of Property Ventures Limited. However, it does highlight what can be achieved in less than 10 years with a starting capital of barely $1.8 million, and copious quantities of energy, enthusiasm, vision, drive, perseverance, and determination.

CHAPTER 20

Never Sell

My constant and frequent encouragement—and even admonishing—to real estate investors never to sell, often seems to fall on either deaf ears or disbelieving ears. For the most part, these investors are seduced by the temptation of a quick profit. It is just one more example of how people tend to think in the short term, rather than the long term. In fact, their thinking is often on such a short time frame that they relish the thought of the profit without fully realizing the imminent tax implications of having made the sale—the ensuing capital gains tax and depreciation recapture tax that must be paid for that financial year.

Unless you live in a country that imposes an *unrealized* capital gains tax on real estate,[1] then so long as you never sell, you never

---

[1]In the United States, there is no capital gains tax on unrealized real estate gains, although unrealized profits on securities held as inventory are taxed.

have to face this tax. Similarly, a depreciation recapture tax is only imposed upon the sale of an asset that has been depreciated.

Those two reasons alone are compelling enough for me, but there is an even more compelling reason not to sell. When you sell a property, you will no longer receive any rent from the property, and you will no longer benefit from the inevitable future capital growth. This reality—that all income from the property will cease the day you sell it—should be a major reason for people not to sell their real estate.

At public events I cajole the audience into coming up with valid reasons to sell a property. Few of the reasons proffered are truly valid. The most common reason given is to take the profit out of an existing investment, and then to use this profit to invest in another property. There are two arguments against this. First, when you sell, as we have seen, you will pay capital gains tax and depreciation recapture tax. Second, while you may release the equity in a property by selling, you could release that same equity by refinancing the property and still retaining it.

For example, imagine you bought a property for $500,000 with a mortgage for $500,000 (you bought it vacant, but with a tenant in place it went up in value and the bank was willing to fund the entire purchase price). Assume it is now worth $2 million. You do not need to sell it to release the $1.5 million of equity. You could achieve the same result by simply refinancing with your existing bank or a new bank. You simply get a new appraisal and submit a new proposal for finance. Now admittedly, if the bank will only go up to a 70 percent loan to value (LTV), then they will only lend you $1.4 million, which is only $900,000 more than your present loan. However, if you sold the property, you would lose perhaps 6 percent in selling commission ($120,000) and at least 15 percent of the capital gain to tax ($225,000), more to depreciation recapture tax, and even more to selling costs, leaving you with perhaps barely a million in net, after-tax profit. Which would you rather have, a million dollars in cash, or equity of $1.5 million (from which you could easily borrow another $900,000), secured against an asset worth $2 million, and rental income for life? The property only has to go up by 5 percent for you to make yet another $100,000 (which would be tax-free so long as you continue not to sell).

The rents and the building value are likely to continue going up. If you wanted cash to buy another building, and instead of selling the existing one you kept it and refinanced it, you could still buy the second property. In this case you would own two buildings that would continue to go up in value.

Here is another situation that some claim justifies selling. Imagine you bought a property for $10 million with a 10 percent return. Assume further that market cap rates have gone down from 10 percent to 5 percent. In this case, the property is now worth $20 million. The argument goes that you should now sell the property, and put the proceeds into another property that may be returning closer to 10 percent again.

The downside of this argument is that cap rates will have gone down if the market has determined that this area has better prospects in terms of rental growth, capital growth, and quality of tenants. By selling this property, and buying one where cap rates are higher—around 10 percent—you are effectively exchanging a property with a great location (hence the 5 percent cap rate) for one with a mediocre location (hence the 10 percent cap rate). Once again, I would say, refinance the existing property and use the proceeds to buy a second one as well.

I cannot keep track of how many times people tell me that they were thrilled to sell a property at a handsome profit, and then a few years later recoiled with total remorse when they realized that the property had doubled or trebled in value yet again. That doubling or trebling in value, if they had kept the property, would have come at the expense of very little marginal effort. There would have been no contracts to study, no due diligence to perform, no finance applications to make—none of the activities normally associated with buying a property. In fact, by not selling the property, they would have saved all the contractual work associated with a sale.

There are, to be sure, extenuating circumstances when there may be some legitimate reasons to sell. For instance, with the restaurant premises that I bought for $120,000 discussed earlier, I had a succession of tenants, and then the building ended up being vacant. After many months of applying all my techniques to attract a tenant, I finally got a call from a couple in Switzerland who were keen to sign up as tenants. I was all excited at the prospect of having the premises leased once more. Then, just before they were going to sign the lease, they contacted me to say that after a lot of thinking, they decided that they would only proceed with their dream of opening their own restaurant if they could own the freehold of the property. I was faced with two options: Hold out for the gamble of a new tenant (which could take a long time), or sell the entire property to the Swiss couple at a handsome profit. It was an easy decision.

The building where the veterinary surgery ended up occupying the premises facing the pedestrian mall is another case in point. I owned that building for 10 years, enjoying an initial income of some $54,000 a year from an investment of $310,000. However, when the veterinarians refused to renew their lease, but offered instead to buy the freehold, I was faced with a similar situation to the one with the restaurant. I could hold on to a building with what would be a 75 percent vacancy in an area of substantial vacancies, or sell the building fully leased, notwithstanding that the buyer was a tenant. Once again I opted to sell.

That is why the rule "Never sell" should perhaps be amended to "Seldom sell." The only reason I am reluctant to do so is to impress upon you that selling should be reserved for exceptional circumstances.

I can count the times I have sold a commercial building I own on the fingers of my hands, and even in some of these cases I have lived to regret it. The only commercial property I have sold in the United States was a small office complex when I needed the proceeds in a hurry for another deal. In a fit of closed-mindedness, I sold this property for $366,000. Today, not five years later, and being located right next to the Phoenix light-rail network, it is appraised at over $800,000. Ouch! Especially when you consider that I had to pay capital gains tax on my $366,000 sale price.

CHAPTER 21

Thirteen Golden Rules of Commercial Real Estate Investment

Golden Rule 1: Risk Is Equal to Yield

As with any endeavor in life, the higher the risk, the higher the reward. To express this using our newfound understanding of cap rates, we would say the lower the risk, the lower the cap rate. In other words, for an investment with low risk, the market capitalizes the rental income with a low cap rate (i.e., a large factor). The market would apply a high cap rate (small factor) to income from a risky property.

Consequently, the aim with real estate is not necessarily to seek the property with the highest return, but rather the property with a good compromise between risk and return that is appropriate (and profitable) for your circumstances.

If you can buy a property with a low risk (low market cap rates) but with a high return, then you have found your deal of the decade.

This leads us to rule number 2.

Golden Rule 2: Ensure Safety of Principal

What is more important, return *on* capital or return *of* capital? What good is an ROI of 25 percent per annum if the investment goes belly-up after two and a half years? Make sure your capital is safe. That includes getting appropriate insurance on your properties so that you will not lose your properties in the event of an earthquake, fire, or other natural causes.

Golden Rule 3: Control Your Liabilities

While in general we have a lot of control over our assets, we have relatively little control over our liabilities. In many parts of the world, it is impossible to fix the interest rate on your mortgage for more than a handful of years. Where you can, make sure you fix the interest rate!

One of the huge advantages of the real estate market in the United States relative to many other countries is that it is possible to obtain mortgages—even 30-year mortgages—where the interest rate is fixed. I am astounded at the number of investors who choose not to fix the rate. For the sake of perhaps a 0.5 percent lower initial interest rate, they are willing to risk interest rates going through the roof in the future. It is a folly not only committed by legions of otherwise sane investors, but also aided and abetted by armies of mortgage brokers who no doubt get a better commission on loans that turn out to be more lucrative for the banks.

Furthermore, you should avoid any requirement for a personal guarantee on any real estate loans. The reasons are twofold. First, a real estate investment should stand up on its own two feet. The risk of having a personal guarantee is that it may be called up, and you would be forced to pay off principal on a loan taken out by an entity with limited liability. Signing a personal guarantee, of course, breaks this liability fire wall.

The second reason why you should avoid any personal guarantees is that when you apply for future loans, banks will often ask for a list of your contingent liabilities—these are liabilities that may end up on your shoulders. The more items in this list, the more reluctant a bank will be to lend you any money.

Golden Rule 4: Add Value to a Deal

If you buy a fully leased commercial property at a fair market price, you are going to have to wait for inflation to increase the value of your rentals and thus the capital value. Alternatively, if you buy a property that has some vacant space, with some rents that are below market, rooftops that are underutilized, storage space that is not leased, and a host of other features that you can do something with, then you can exchange your ideas, thoughts, energy, and enthusiasm for huge chunks of capital value very quickly. In other words, *you* are an extremely important factor in the real estate you acquire.

Another way of expressing this is to say that when I buy a property, it is a different property from when you buy it. Physically it is the exact same property, but since the ideas that I bring to the table are likely to be different from the ideas that you bring to the table, the property itself ends up being different. Whether you like it or not, you end up being part of the equation. That is why the more ideas you have in your head, the more value you add. That is how I came up with another signature statement:

The most valuable piece of real estate is the six inches, give or take an inch or two, between your right ear and your left ear. What you create in that space determines your ultimate wealth and happiness.

Golden Rule 5: A Broker or Agent Must Bring Something to the Deal

Just as you become part of the equation, your broker or buyer's agent must also bring something to the deal. Remember, in most parts of the world, the selling commission is paid for by the seller. If you choose to enlist the services of a buyer's agent, make sure they contribute something of value other than an e-mail with present listings. Agents with whom I have worked over time know to bring me not just real estate listings but background information, pending zone changes, ideas for alternative uses, and even prospective tenants. Furthermore, they willingly go to this extra effort, as they know doing so will result in more deals being closed and therefore more commission to them.

Golden Rule 6: Real Estate Is a Long-Term Investment

One of the aspects of commercial real estate that I particularly enjoy is that you can buy a property, have some rudimentary management in place, and then all but forget about it. In fact, you could take a six-month cruise and not worry on a day-to-day basis whether everything is all right. If you need more nail-biting, nerve-racking excitement than that, then trade stocks, where you generally have to monitor the market by the day; or trade options, where you have to monitor the market by the hour; or trade futures, where you have to monitor the market by the minute; or trade currencies or other derivatives, where you have to monitor the market by the second.

Also take note that you will not find many stock traders over 50, many options traders over 40, many currency traders over 30, or many futures traders over 25. These nail-biting, glued-to-your-screen professions burn people out. They also require that their practitioners complete another deal to earn another dollar of income.

Meanwhile, back on your cruise boat, you are reading books or mingling with people, knowing that your tenants will pay rent that month whether you have worked or not.

Seen in this light, I again make a comment on something to which I have already devoted an entire chapter: Never sell. When you sell, you lose your income stream from an asset that is rising steadily in value.

Golden Rule 7: The Number of Voting Partners Is Directly Proportional to the Failure of the Project

This rule is almost self-explanatory. It is a variation on the cliché that too many cooks spoil the broth. We saw that the original 10 investors behind the Spring Mountain water-ski lake project had a falling-out, which led them to sell the project at its original cost price. Taken to its extreme, the best way to avoid project failures through disagreements is to undertake all projects alone. However, there are always economies of scale and great synergies of ideas when you team up with others. The trick is, as with all things in life, to find a good balance between a free flow of many ideas, and impasses through disagreements.

Golden Rule 8: You Are Going to Be in a Lawsuit

Whether you are averse to litigation or not, sooner or later you will end up being in a lawsuit. Stay in good communication with people, and try to think outside the box to come up with a solution that may be beneficial to everyone (and a lot cheaper in the long run). A perfect example is the situation with the 10-foot strip of land that I thought I owned, but did not through negligence on many people's part. While I could have litigated, I didn't want the wasted time, energy, expense, or uncertainty of that option.

Rather, I came to an agreement with the other innocent party (the neighbor) that was beneficial to everyone.

Golden Rule 9: It Only Takes One Deal to Go Broke

An accident generally comes about not because one major thing goes wrong, but rather because a whole series of seemingly unrelated things come together at the same time to cause the catastrophic event. In the case of real estate, interest rates might move up a bit, tenant demand goes down, your space becomes a little obsolete through new technology, a freeway bypasses your side of town, an airline drops your local airport as a hub, and all of a sudden you are facing a crisis that six months prior you had not envisaged, and which any one of these changes in isolation would not have caused.

Never become complacent. Always keep your finger on what is happening in the market. Try to deal with all challenges as they arise, and not as they come together to cause a big event. Fix your interest rates, keep your buildings modern by incorporating new technology, and find out how to keep your tenants happy with the premises they lease.

Golden Rule 10: It Only Takes One Deal to Make a Million Dollars

Just as it takes only one deal to go broke, you can also make a million dollars from a single deal. When it comes to commercial real estate, it is not always a numbers game, where the more properties you buy, the greater the chance you have of becoming financially free. While in general two deals are better than one, you would be far better off working on one commercial property and managing it efficiently and properly, rather than taking on five projects and barely being able to keep up with which tenant owes how much in rent.

Golden Rule 11: The Value of a Property Is Limited by the Tenant's Ability to Pay Rent

This rule is just another way of defining the cap rate. If you cannot find a tenant for a building, then your building will not be worth very much, and no banker will lend you any money to buy or refinance it. Your ability to acquire a portfolio, and the subsequent value of that portfolio, depends on your ability to secure stable, long-term tenants.

More particularly, the value of a building is not just dependent on what you manage to get one tenant to pay in rent. What if you lost that one high-rent tenant? The value of a building is dependent on what rent you could get any tenant to pay within a reasonable time span. Therefore, always work on improving the environment for existing tenants—it will make them reluctant to leave. Then, if they do leave, it will be all the easier to find replacement tenants.

Golden Rule 12: Appreciation and Inflation Are Compounded Annually

While appreciation increases the value of your portfolio, inflation erodes the value of money. This is supremely beneficial for real estate investors.

Assume you have a portfolio worth $10 million, with a mortgage of $9 million. Let's also assume that over time—for the sake of this argument it matters not how much time—the portfolio appreciates to $20 million. This does not mean that the $9 million mortgage appreciated to $18 million. The asset may have appreciated, but the loan was expressed in dollars, and at worst (interest only) it stayed at $9 million. Furthermore, through inflation, that $9 million will be easier to pay off (it is effectively worth less than it was before).

This is one of the prime reasons why you are in real estate. These factors work even when you don't. Meanwhile, flippers, traders, and speculators have to keep on working to earn their next dollar.

Golden Rule 13: You Cannot Give Kindness Away—It Is Always Returned

You cannot beat a crook—even with a team of great lawyers, real estate agents, accountants, private detectives, and other professionals. Even if you successfully litigate, and you get what you think you are owed, the crooks will have taken something else somewhere else along the way, not to mention all the wasted time, effort, and energy that you put into dealing with these people in the first place, and then cleaning up the mess they precipitated.

There is only one solution: Deal with ethical people. You may not make money as fast, but it will last longer, and you will feel better about it.

One tremendous advantage of dealing with ethical people is that they tend to hang around with other ethical people. Your circle of acquaintances spirals into more and more enlightened levels of fairness, kindness, and awareness. Conversely, when you hang with rogues and rascals, your circle of acquaintances tends to spiral into depraved levels of increasingly severe cheating and deception.

Remember, you become the company you keep, so choose your friends and associates very carefully. John Baen is not only one of the most knowledgeable people I know concerning real estate, but he has a heart of gold. That is not to say he is weak—never confuse kindness for weakness.

Be firm about your expectations. Most disagreements come about because of a mismatch of expectations between two parties. Therefore, be aware of your own expectations and, equally important, discuss them with your associates. If you discover a chasm between your way of doing things and that of some associates, turn them into former associates. The world is too full of interesting, kind, knowledgeable, and energetic people to be bothered wasting time with takers, no matter how fancy the cars they drive or the homes they live in.

CHAPTER 22

Investing Abroad

A tremendous advantage of being a passionate real estate investor is that you can indulge in your hobby all over the world.

Think about this: A physician usually studies at a university for five years or so, and then completes two or three more years of residency, before becoming a fully qualified doctor, licensed to practice *only in the country in which he gained his qualifications*. This doctor cannot decide to move to another country and set up shop with a sign above his door saying, "Fully qualified doctor available for medical interventions." He would be arrested by the local authorities, even though he spent all those years studying and becoming qualified in another country, and despite the fact that his subject matter—human bodies—is essentially identical all over the world, with a few variations on skin hue, average height, and eating habits.

Not only can our doctor friend not move to another country

and ply his trade, he cannot even go somewhere for two weeks or even one day and legally perform an appendectomy, lobotomy, or tonsillectomy without running afoul of the local medical governing body. Whether rules preventing physicians from practicing in other countries are justified or not (it can be difficult to verify the authenticity of some foreign qualifications, and there are plenty of examples of horrific consequences of sloppy checking), the reality is that a physician is generally confined to practicing in the country in which he studied.

Doctors can, of course, complete whatever training is required by a new country and qualify there, but often the effort is too onerous. A good friend of mine was one of Austria's top dermatologists but, upon emigrating to Melbourne, Australia, found the requirements to requalify there so onerous and time consuming that he became a pig farmer instead—a very successful and happy one at that.

In a similar vein, dentists, anesthetists, pilots, attorneys, psychologists, psychiatrists, military personnel, and even real estate agents cannot simply go to another country, either permanently or on a working holiday, and legally ply their trade without requalification. Sometimes the rules are so different in another country that it would genuinely be difficult to work there without retraining (such as with law), and sometimes the governing bodies just exclude outsiders. The net effect is the same, however: Many professions do not allow for the possibility of working wherever and for however long you want in another country.

This contrasts greatly with real estate investing, where not only are there no legal restrictions on operating your profession in another country, but most countries welcome you with open arms on the basis that you will be bringing investment funds to their region. Even when they know you borrow most of your funds locally, they still welcome you with open arms, as you are generating business across the board with your activities.

The chambers of commerce of many countries put on events all over the world to lure investors to their countries. In many countries, when you go there and reveal that you are an investor, you will be treated with respect and given a lot of support and assistance. When you have invested in a country, you will often be treated like royalty and offered even more investments that may not already be publicly available. And when you have invested sufficiently in some countries, you will get invitations to advise them, joint-venture with them, or sit on their corporate boards. What a sharp contrast to other professions!

A few people have admonished me for suggesting investors look beyond their own borders, claiming that real estate is so complex, and that the laws regarding real estate are so involved, that it is difficult to keep up with the regulations in your own turf, let alone in a foreign country. Consequently, they claim, investing overseas is risky and foolish, and I am just grandstanding or showing off by talking about investing internationally.

Well, let's consider a few alternative attitudes. First, few people living in the United States realize this, but the value of the U.S. dollar, when measured against a trade-weighted basket of currencies, has fallen in the seven years since the year 2000 by a massive 58 percent (as tourists traveling to Europe are finding out through the increased cost of a vacation there). In other words, if you had shipped $1 million overseas with the intent of investing it in real estate, but you never quite got around to making the investment, and today you repatriated the funds back to the United States, you would have more than $2 million. I have investors who took my advice and invested in New Zealand at a time when a United

States dollar bought NZ$2.40. Today, that same NZ$2.40 buys over US$1.90. In other words, the value of their investment has nearly doubled without even taking into account how the investment in New Zealand has fared.

Bear in mind that one of the tremendous advantages of real estate is that you do not need most of the money required to buy a property—banks willingly provide those funds in the form of a mortgage. In general, banks will not lend money on real estate purchased abroad,[1] so if you were to buy a NZ$10 million property in New Zealand, you may only need NZ$1 million or less as a down payment from your own country—the rest is financed locally. If the value of this investment over time goes from NZ$10 million to NZ$20 million, then not only have you made a 1,000 percent return on your cash investment of NZ$1 million, but the NZ$10 million profit, expressed in U.S. dollars, will also have gone up (or down) according to the change in exchange rate.

Secondly, many people claim that investing overseas is unpatriotic, as it diverts resources away from your home country to other countries. This is pure nonsense for two reasons. As we have just been reminded, when you invest in real estate in a foreign country, most of the funds required for an acquisition are provided by a locally sourced mortgage. Furthermore, claiming that investing abroad diverts funds away from your own country ignores the fact that the explicit purpose of any investment is to generate a return and (should you ever sell) a capital profit, both of which will eventually be brought back to your country.

We can illustrate this last point using Great Britain as an ex-

---

[1]One exception that I have only discovered in the past few months is specific U.S. banks willing to lend money to U.S. residents to acquire real estate in Mexico.

ample. With all due respect to that country, and without wanting to offend my many friends there, there is little that comes out of Great Britain these days that is coveted by the rest of the world. British cars do not have the appeal or following of their German or Japanese counterparts. The country is not known as a hotbed of fashion. You would not vacation there on account of the climate. The London Underground is not exactly a showpiece of technological marvels. And you would certainly not consider Great Britain as the culinary center of the world. What have you recently bought that is British?

Based on this simplistic analysis, the country should not be doing very well at all economically, and yet the gross domestic product (GDP) is robust and strong. The reason, of course, is the so-called invisible income that Great Britain derives from more than a century of having made judicious and fortuitous investments abroad. Take the insurance industry, for instance. Great Britain controls more than 70 percent of the reinsurance industry, largely through the operations of Lloyd's of London (with Switzerland mopping up most of the remaining 30 percent). Britain similarly has substantial investments abroad in banking, pharmaceuticals, and transportation, to name a few. No doubt the Brits making these investments 100 years ago were also branded as being unpatriotic, as they were taking pounds sterling out of their country back then, but the entire nation is now benefiting from the ongoing repatriation to Great Britain of dividends, profits, rents, and realized capital gains.

Just how do these repatriated profits benefit the entire nation rather than just the companies and individuals controlling the investments? First, on entering the country, these funds push up the value of the British pound. And once the profits are in the coffers of a recipient company, that company will tend to spend the money in a number of different ways. They will invest some into research and development, employing scientists, engineers, physicists, chemists, and a slew of technical support staff. They will conduct marketing surveys and advertising campaigns, employing PR firms, communications experts, marketing staff, and legal spin doctors. They may expand their premises, employing architects, engineers, construction workers, electricians, plumbers, painters, and the like. I think you get the picture. Money coming into a country tends to end up benefiting everyone. Money leaving a country tends to disadvantage everyone. That is why a balance of trade surplus is so healthy for a country, and a deficit is so debilitating.

Consequently, when you invest abroad, you are doing your bit (and a lot more than most people) to benefit your country for generations to come. Do not let any simple-minded, envious critic make you feel in the least awkward about investing in real estate abroad.

There is another aspect of investing abroad that I feel is worth mentioning. Many people work very hard at a job, earning a gross income. From this gross income, tax is deducted and then, with what is left, they pay their accommodation (rent or a mortgage), food, gas, electricity, clothing, entertainment, medical and dental expenses, schooling for kids, and a slew of other household outgoings. The little that is left is saved, some for a rainy day, some for a new car, and some for the annual vacation.

Let's talk about this annual vacation. Let's say you end up in some fabulous beach resort, in a suite overlooking the sea, where you can enjoy beautiful sunsets while savoring the in-room dining. Unbeknownst to you, I could be in a suite not too far away, enjoying essentially the same view and virtually the same sunset, and savoring food from the same menu. However, my stay may not have been paid out of the meager savings left over after paying taxes and all household expenses. My trip (not vacation) will in all probability have been paid out of pretax dollars.

Here is the reason. In my quest to find great real estate deals, to find material for my columns and articles, to find locations and topics to film for my weekly real estate videos *Discussions with Dolf*, and to research material for books, I travel to many places around the world. I try to add at least one country every year to the list of countries I have visited, a list that now exceeds 94 countries.

Last month I went to Poland for the first time, meeting up with software engineers who have been working on a project for us, seeing firsthand the effects of 60 years of Stalinist and Communist repression on the real estate industry, and finding out how in the past decade and in anticipation of Poland joining the European Union, prices of real estate went up by a *factor* of 20. During my visit, I came across tour buses full of tourists who get to see the country from the cocoon of a bus, surrounded by fellow countrymen, all knowing that they must finish breakfast and be ready to board the bus by 7:30 P.M. each morning or it will leave without them. That is not an interesting way to experience a country, let alone to meet the locals to find out what makes them tick. Travel alone or with a loved one, have a purpose, throw fate into the wind, and be open to new discoveries. Avoid itineraries, advanced hotel bookings, or even advanced dinner reservations—they can stifle creativity, a fortuitous meeting, and, most important, the serendipitous acquisition of a prime piece of real estate.

While a lack of background knowledge and experience in a foreign market can appear to be a disadvantage, there is also a commensurate advantage: Your opinion as to whether a deal is great or not isn't clouded by knowledge of past events related to the building or area.

A few years back I was shown a property by Craig Donnell, a colleague who consistently ferrets out opportunistic deals, in Melbourne, Australia. The building was located directly opposite the

University of Melbourne, and comprised 12 stories of student accommodation (277 rooms) along with ground-floor retail space and a basement. (See Figure 22.1.) There was a new 10-plus-5-plus-5-year lease in place to the university at a starting rental of A$950,000 per annum, with annual reviews in line with the consumer price index (CPI). To an outsider looking at market cap rates, returns, location, strength of lease, and in deference to the fact that the building had been completely renovated, it appeared as though the building was being offered at a price substantially above market. This would also explain why it had not sold.

However, this building also highlights the need to conduct thorough due diligence. It turns out that despite the recent renovations, the building did not comply with the fire code. Before long, the students had to be evacuated and relocated, and the university commenced legal action against the owner. We were informed that an offer would be entertained by the owner, who was eager to extricate himself from the situation.

To locals, the uncertain status of the lease (given the legal action) was a disadvantage. To us, the building could realistically be rented out under independent management for closer to A$2.5 million per annum. Consequently, we were negotiating at a price less than half the original asking price (because of the local market discounting the price on account of an uncertain lease), when in actual fact it was worth more to us *without* a lease. Furthermore, we knew that the cost of bringing the building up to fire code was nowhere near the millions we would save in acquisition costs.

However, just as you can own a property in an instant, so can you lose the opportunity. Despite the validity of the lease still being in question, a group of attorneys bought the building (for far more than our offer), partially negating my claim that locals often

Figure 22.1   Student Accommodation Opposite the University of Melbourne

discount a property beyond reason, but at the same time raising the question as to whether they paid too much for it.

A foreigner is more likely to look at a property on the basis of the facts—what is the market value, the market rental, capital growth rate, rental growth, vacancy rate, and so forth—than a local. A local will be more inclined to take into account sentiments such as, "Well, this suburb has never really been that popular except with people on government subsidies" or some such nonsense. I say nonsense, because once the profits are in your bank account, it no longer matters whether they came from a popular suburb or an unpopular one. In fact, cap rates will be lower in popular suburbs—the market has already taken account of everything for you.

Furthermore, by investing abroad, not only can you get the benefit of a cross-fertilization of ideas, but you can also benefit from a cross-fertilization of projects. In New Zealand I am involved with a boutique hotel and a small vineyard. To many people, this may just be of passing interest, but my colleague and friend Rich Lamphere recognized a tremendous opportunity to link the New Zealand operation to his extensive project in northern California that also includes a vineyard and boutique hotel. Rich is a true visionary with a big heart, and is living proof of Zig Ziglar's maxim that "You can get whatever you want, so long as you help enough other people get what they want." By offering guests in either country wines from both projects, reciprocal hotel perks, combined frequent-user benefits, and an excuse and incentives to use the other country's facilities, both projects benefit.

As for the claim that real estate is so complex, and the laws so involved, that it is difficult to keep up with the regulations in your own turf, let alone a foreign country, these critics need to get a passport (I would put money on it that they do not have one), jump on a plane, and go somewhere where they have never been before. Of course real estate is complex, even at home. In fact, it is so complex that even at home you should barely do any of it yourself.

Engage real estate agents to handle the contract for sale and purchase of the property. Engage attorneys to go over lease documents. Engage engineers, geologists, surveyors, and inspectors to help with the due diligence. Engage title companies to transfer (or convey) the title from the seller to you. Engage CPAs to do the accounting to conform to local taxation regulations. Even though it is perfectly legal to perform most of these tasks yourself (and at some stage you probably should, just to find out what is involved) in general you would be a fool to attempt any of these things on your own in your own country, especially since it is so easy to find people to do these things for you. In a similar vein, you would be a fool to attempt any of these things in a foreign country, and again it is so easy to find people to do these things for you.

Investing abroad may stretch your comfort zone from time to time, but so what if things are a bit different? It adds to the spice of life. They may drive on the other side of the road—no big deal. They may have a different mains voltage, frequency, and plug configuration. Bring some adaptors or buy what you need locally. Traffic lights may have different sequences (for instance, red and amber may come on simultaneously prior to going green). At least red, amber, and green lights are standard around the world! They may have different currencies, computer keyboard layouts, and customs. Bring it all on! So what if a sidewalk is called a footpath, a trunk is called a boot, and a hood is called a bonnet? Similarly, so what if title is not transferred at a title company, but rather conveyed by a conveyancing solicitor, with *solicitor* meaning attorney? A great deal is still a great deal, no matter what voltage is powering the universal power supply to your notebook.

If critics admonish you for investing abroad, let them wallow in their own ignorance. They probably also think that everyone in the world should speak their language, drive on their side of the road, and be grateful to them for something. But, as my friend John Baen keeps saying, it's not who's right, but what's right. Investing abroad benefits everyone, including the very critics who would like to take you to task for being so selfish, unpatriotic, and crazy as to invest beyond your own borders.

CHAPTER 23

Live Life to the Fullest

Most people, when asked, will agree that the real estate industry is huge. Few, however, have ever stopped to think just how large it is. When you consider that almost everyone lives in a home, be it owner-occupied or a rental, that adds up to a lot of real estate. Furthermore, every supermarket that we shop at, school that we attend or send our kids to, hotel that we stay at, airport that we use, computer store that we drop by at, coffee shop that we indulge at, gas station where we fill our cars, movie theater that we frequent, restaurant that we dine at, and so on and so forth, all these venues host businesses that fuel the economy and are operated out of real estate premises. Seen in its entirety, the real estate market, both in capital value terms and in rental value terms, is singularly and definitively the largest industry there is.

Given that the industry is so incredibly large, it follows that there are many ways to be involved in real estate. You may, for instance, think you are not directly involved in real estate at all, noting that you rent your apartment and work as an employee at a flower delivery company. Of course, in this case, you are renting your home (and thus you are an obvious participant in the real estate industry). Further, your employer rents or owns the premises you work out of, and someone owns the garages where the delivery trucks are serviced, as well as the yard in which the trucks are stored overnight. The flowers you deliver are grown in someone's commercial premises, and they are transported to your employer's warehouse using vehicles—trains or planes that each require millions of dollars of real estate to operate fully. Everyone is at the very least a user of real estate, even if the use is passive and merely the consequence of another activity.

You may also be more directly involved in the real estate industry. For instance, you could work at a title company, for a building inspection firm, or as an appraiser, real estate attorney, loan officer, mortgage originator, mortgage broker, real estate agent, real estate broker, real estate expert witness, real estate professor, construction worker, telephone line installer, or at a myriad of other professions all servicing the real estate industry. These services have one thing in common, and that is that they do not involve direct ownership of real estate.

Rather than being involved in the periphery of real estate, you could be a real estate speculator, trader, flipper, or developer, as indeed many tens of thousands of people are, and take ownership, at some stage, of the real estate you are dealing with.

The point is, of the thousands of potential occupations associated with real estate including all the ones just listed, this

book addresses none of them. This book has been purely ai
at investors.[1]

Even within the realm of investing in real estate, there are
two main approaches. The first approach, adopted by most individual investors and almost all institutional investors, is to buy a
property at a fair market value and then sit on it for a long time,
waiting for inflation and a general improvement in the economy
to increase rentals and, as a result, the capital value of the real estate. This book is also not for this category of investor.

This book has singularly focused on finding a property with a
twist, with an anomaly that you can use to your advantage (and
the advantage of your tenant—it's a win-win, remember). By finding a property with a wacky element—it may be that there is an
imminent zone change, or you can convert warehouse space to retail space, or you can add a floor, or sell air rights, or put in a helipad, or whatever—you can massively increase the value in a short
space of time.

Apart from the fact that this form of investing is mathemati-
cally far more efficient and lucrative than just sitting back and waiting for inflation to do its job, there is another tremendous advantage
that I have not yet highlighted, and that is that it is a lot of fun.

There are in general three categories of people. Simple people
talk about other people. A meeting with them will involve such in-
tellectually stimulating discussions as, "Did you see what so-and-
so was wearing at the party last night? How do they pluck up the

---

[1]Note that speculating, trading, flipping, and developing are not investment
activities; they may be legitimate ways of making money through real estate,
but in my opinion the practitioners are definitely not investors. An investment must be, among other things, passive and generate passive income,
thereby disqualifying these four activities.

courage? And you should have heard what so-and-so had to say about it! Not that they have any right to talk, given what they have been seen wearing at times." Enough said.

The second category of people talk not about other people but about things. A conversation with them may involve snippets like, "Can you believe what is going on in Iraq? Just what is the outcome going to be? And what about that hurricane that just blew through the Caribbean? You know, they say that hurricanes are becoming more frequent these days with global warming. Makes you wonder where it is all leading. I sure hope insurance companies will pay out this time after the hurricane, though."

Hmmm. Let's move on to the third category!

The third category of people tend to talk about neither people nor things, but rather about ideas. They are the creative ones exploring the outer limits of what is possible, of what may be. They are the ones who keep you awake at night, as you ponder what it was they said, whether it is possible, and how you may participate.

Ross, Randy, and I were returning from a trip to our water-ski lakes by helicopter, and on landing at Chandler Municipal Airport we met Steve Fossett, who was getting out of his helicopter. (See Figure 23.1.) At that stage Steve already held 106 world records in five sports. He had completed the first solo circumnavigation of the world without refueling, in 67 hours in the Virgin Atlantic GlobalFlyer. He was the first person to fly a balloon solo around the world. That day he was completing helicopter training for a new endeavor. Steve is, of course, an inspiration just with what he has achieved, and a meeting with him makes you dream big about your own ventures and ponder what it is you are doing with your own life.

A few weeks later I was on a Virgin Atlantic flight from Los Angeles to London. The pilot, Alex Tai, came out of his fortified

Figure 23.1   **Dolf with Steve Fossett and Randy Carder**

cockpit to chat with me (gone, since 9/11, are the days when I would get to sit with them). When I mentioned that I had just met with Steve Fossett in Arizona, he replied, "No kidding? I was the pilot of the chase plane for his around-the world flight." Captain Tai is also the chief pilot for Virgin Galactic, set to be the first commercial operation to offer members of the public flights into outer space from the company's base in New Mexico.

"Maybe," said Captain Tai, "you can help us acquire the land for our launch pad in New Mexico. And you absolutely should be one of the first to come into space with us."

That last sentence only comprised 15 words, but the effect on me was profound. I was not reading about the commercialization of space flights in *Newsweek* or *Time* magazine or the *Economist*.

Rather, I was face-to-face with the opportunity to be one of the first to leave our planet on a commercial operation.

And here is the point. Real estate investors are for the most part and by their nature in the third category of people who talk about what is possible, and who come up with creative solutions to common problems. Whether real estate investing attracts this category of upbeat, thinking people, or whether the nature of the work turns ordinary ho-hum people into go-getters, I do not know and do not really care. The fact remains that real estate investors are, in general, a pretty motivated, excitable, and exciting bunch of people to hang with. That is why I say that this branch of the real estate industry is a lot of fun.

My experiences when I was studying for my PhD are a good point of comparison. The academic world is largely one of "publish or perish"—your job offers, tenure, reputation, and therefore income are largely dependent on how many good academic papers you publish in the scientific literature. As a result, every scientist is fiercely protective of his work, hoping to be the first one to publish it and therefore lay claim to the underlying technology or ideas.

Consequently, the conferences I attended showed considerable rivalry between individual academics, groups of academics, and even students and their supervisors. Conferences had an aura of suspicion, jealousy, and one-upmanship.

This contrasts dramatically with the real estate investment industry. At conferences I have attended, there is a jovial underlying atmosphere, and a free flow of information and ideas that is contagious. Unlike in the scientific world, investors want to share their techniques with you. After all, if it's a great technique, why not share it?

I am not at all worried that if I share my real estate ideas in this book, there will be no good deals left for me. Again, the market is so incredibly huge, with just about every human being on this planet (and there are now well over six billion of them) using dozens of forms of real estate every single day, that there will still be plenty of deals for me to work with. My signature statement is still true, namely that the deal of the decade comes along about once a week.

For me, real estate investing is not just about doing the deal. If that were all there was to it, then I would just stay in one location, say Phoenix, which has about the highest growth rate of any indicator you care to monitor anywhere in the world, and consummate deal after deal. However, human beings also have a hankering for some variety.

Saint Augustine is credited with saying, "The world is a book, and he who does not travel reads only one page." Travel to broaden your horizons, for the sheer joy of it, and to get new ideas. I have transplanted countless ideas from one part of the world to another, and these ideas simply would not even have occurred to me if I had not traveled. It was my observation of the efficiency of Japanese car-parking systems that enabled me to make otherwise dysfunctional office buildings work in other parts of the world. It was seeing how, all over Europe, people live, work, and play in a mixed-use environment that led to an affinity with new urbanism, which got incorporated into numerous projects. It was the sourcing of reliable electronics in Thailand that led to the complete automation of buildings in Australia. It was teaming up with an investor from the United States who wanted to hedge against a falling U.S. dollar that enabled me to be involved with building the largest private medical facility in New Zealand.

When you travel, you also get to meet some very colorful and interesting people. It will broaden your circle of friends and the pool of information you can learn from.

The clichés are true: "You become the company you keep." "Birds of a feather flock together." "The quality of a person's life is in direct proportion to the quality of their peer group." Therefore, choose your friends carefully. Sometimes, fire some of your friends. If you are the smartest person on your team, then your team is in trouble!

The great thing about commercial real estate investing is that the people involved are largely preselected (or they have been transformed from their prior state of complacency). You won't need to fire many of them as your friends, as they are all already upbeat, motivated, eager to learn, and knowledgeable.

When I say "knowledgeable," I mean that you can learn something from them. Investors are happy to share their knowledge. As I stated right at the beginning of this book, learn something new every day. When I teach at an event with 2,000 people, I have the advantage, as the audience only gets to learn from one person, but I get to learn from 2,000 at a time. I don't say this lightly or to pander. My teachings are very interactive, and I get a lot of feedback—and ideas—from the audience.

Strive to see things from a different angle. Don't just do what other people do simply because "everyone else is doing it that way." Dare to be different. The more you are willing to stand out from the crowd, the more fun you will have, and the greater will be your success at investing in commercial real estate.

Successful investing!

About the Author

Dr. Dolf de Roos began investing in real estate as an undergraduate student. Despite going on to earn a PhD in electrical and electronic engineering from the University of Canterbury, Dolf increasingly focused on his flair for real estate investing, which has enabled him to have never had a job. He has, however, invested in many types of real estate (residential, commercial, industrial, hospitality, and specialist) all over the world.

Today he is the chairman of the public company Property Ventures Limited, an innovative real estate investment company whose stated aim is to massively increase stockholders' worth. He is also a director of Best Choice Properties, an Arizona-based investment company.

Dolf was cajoled into sharing his investment strategies, and he has run seminars on the psychology of creating wealth and on real estate investing throughout North America, Australia, New Zealand, Asia, South Africa, the Middle East, and Europe since the 1980s. He has been appointed a visiting professor of real estate at the University of Texas, and he teaches real estate at Trump University and Tony Robbins' Wealth Mastery.

Beyond sharing his investment philosophy and strategies with tens of thousands of investors (beginners as well as seasoned experts), Dolf has also trained real estate agents, written and published numerous best-selling books on property (including the *New York Times* best seller *Real Estate Riches*), and introduced computer software designed to analyze and manage properties quickly and efficiently. He often speaks at investors' conferences, real estate agents' conventions, and his own international seminars, and regularly takes part in radio shows and television debates. Born in New Zealand, and raised in Australia, New Zealand, and Europe, Dolf, with six languages up his sleeve, offers a truly global perspective on the surprisingly lucrative wealth-building opportunities of real estate.

To find out what you can learn from Dolf's willingness to share his knowledge about creating wealth through real estate, and to receive his free monthly newsletter, please visit his web site: www.dolfderoos.com.

Appendix

Resources

Other Books by Dolf de Roos

Tax-Free Real Estate Investments

In this enlightening money-saving guide, you will learn all the tax-busting secrets financial planners keep to themselves, including how to use a real estate IRA to combine the tax benefits of retirement savings with the high rates of appreciation in real estate investing to grow your savings at light speed.

52 Homes in 52 Weeks

A real estate guide unlike any other, this book is the true story of a seemingly impossible investing challenge and two investors who pulled it off—all to prove that you can do it, too.

Real Estate Riches

This book will show you why real estate is tens and hundreds of times better than other investments. It will prepare you to find the deal of the decade—that comes along every week. Also, learn how the tax man can subsidize your real estate investment. Most importantly, this book will reveal how you can create passive income using your banker's money so you only work if you want to! Rerelease with foreword written by baseball superstar Alex Rodriguez.

Making Money in Real Estate

This book explains why real estate is a consistently profitable moneymaker and how everyday people just like you can build their fortune regardless of their credit score or how much money they have in the bank. It's true—you don't have to be rich to invest in real estate. It's the easiest, most leveraged method for building sustainable wealth over time, and it's open to everyone.

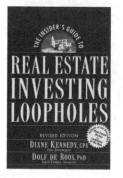

Real Estate Investing Loopholes

This book reveals the best and most effective tax loopholes successful real estate investors use to maximize their profits. This revised edition covers all the new tax laws, and features new and updated case studies and examples. Find out why real estate is probably the best investment money can buy, due in part to the profit-maximizing tax loopholes that directly benefit real estate investors.

Building Wealth Through Investment Property

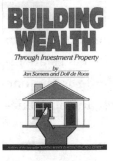

If you want to leave your retirement security in the hands of someone else and are prepared to settle for a whole lot less, this book is not for you.

The wealth-building strategy outlined in this book is not new, it's not complicated, and it's not a get-rich-quick scheme. What it does offer is a reliable path to financial independence in 10 years or even less, by investing in residential property and using the equity in your own home.

Extraordinary Profits

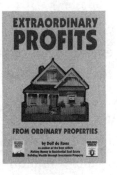

This book is filled with real stories, many with pictures, submitted by people recounting their personal real estate triumphs as they turned ordinary properties into extraordinary profits. This collection of unique, interesting, and at times amazing examples is sure to inspire you to see the possibility in your everyday surroundings.

Making Money in Residential Real Estate

This *Investor's Guide to Making Money in Residential Real Estate* is the answer to your dreams. It tells you everything you need to know to secure your personal financial independence, and does so in a very understandable, easy-to-follow way.

Making Money will show you how to achieve financial security by investing long-term in income-producing residential property. The strategy described here places emphasis on diverting short-term income into long-term asset building so that when your working life stops, your income doesn't.

Real Estate Investment & Management

The SuccessDNA Guide to Real Estate Investment & Management offers practical information on the essential elements of real estate acquisition and ownership, written in a clear and understandable style by two real estate investors and best-selling authors. This guide is the one you will keep and refer to many times over, to your benefit and advantage.

101 Ways to Massively Increase the Value of Your Real Estate without Spending Much Money

101 Ways to Massively Increase the Value of Your Real Estate provides just that: 101 property improvement ideas you can apply to your investment in order to transform the initial impression people get from your property. Transform a so-so property to a *wow!* property without spending tons of money. By utilizing any number of these suggestions, you will improve the rental value, rentability, market value, sale price, and equity of your real estate investment. This is the book to help you get the maximum profit on your investment.

Audio Courses by Dolf de Roos

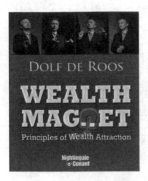

Wealth Magnet (7-CD set, workbook)

Wealthy people have a much better strategy for having it all. It's not so much that they do things differently; it's that they have a different psychology. With *Wealth Magnet*, you can get the tools you need so you can replicate this psychology and achieve wealth beyond your wildest dreams. This breakthrough information can be applied by anyone.

You will learn:

- Why it's crucial to eliminate destructive beliefs such as "Money can't buy you happiness" and "Money is the root of all evil," and replace them with empowering beliefs like "Money gives me choices."

- The critical difference between an abundance mentality and a scarcity mentality—and how to develop and apply an abundance mentality right away.

- Why scrimping and saving is a defensive strategy to grow wealth—and why it's much better to expand your opportunities and create wealth in abundance.

- How your newfound millionaire mind-set will make every aspect of your life richer—you'll discover more opportunities to create value, to make contributions to others, and to express gratitude for the abundance you already have in your life.

- The difference between good and bad debt—and how to use debt to your advantage rather than being a victim of it.

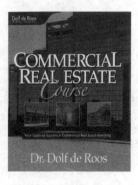

**Commercial Real Estate Course
(12-CD set, workbook)**

Dolf presents his acclaimed commercial real estate semi-nar, designed to show you the ins and outs of investing in commercial real estate. If you are investing in residen-tial property, or have started to invest in commercial property and want to take your investing to the next level, this course is for you. Discover the differences be-tween commercial and residential real estate, and why commercial should be the next step for you.

You will learn:

- How to source commercial property, and what to look for.
- Which market sector is best for you—retail, office, indus-trial, hospitality, or specialist?
- How to double or triple the value of a commercial building before you buy it.
- Why commercial property can be a safer bet for many investors.
- Understanding yield, capital growth, and cap rates.
- How to find tenants and avoid long periods of vacancies.
- Steps to financing your investments.
- What to include in your proposal to make a convincing pitch to banks.
- The dos and don'ts of managing property.
- Should you use a property manager?
- How to set up your corporate structure to protect your assets.
- Tax advantages available through commercial investing.

**Property Investor's School
(10-CD set)**

Property Investor's School (PIS) is a live recording of our unique two-day event, which is only available to a select number of participants in any year. Professionally recorded and edited, this course will provide you with the knowledge and confidence to easily create passive income through real estate. While there can be no substitute for attending our live event, this recording is the next best thing. In fact, our participants who have listened to the program prior to attending the event greatly increase what they learn and retain.

The program refers to a "Proposal for Finance" document that is available on the web site. You may view it and download it by going to www.dolfderoos.com. Of course, if you do not yet have the audio set, you can still view the "Proposal for Finance" but you won't get the benefit of the detailed explanations.

Included: *Property Investor's Guidebook*—an interactive 100-plus-page workbook designed to be used in conjunction with the audio portion of the *PIS*, allowing you to work along with Dolf as he takes you through individual investment processes.

Software by Dolf de Roos

REAP is the most powerful property analysis tool of its kind. It was developed to enable users throughout the world to analyze the investment value of real estate. You will learn to consistently identify lucrative investments and, more important, avoid bad ones. You will be able to focus on the best opportunities with the strongest growth potential—the ones that will actually make you money each week, month, or year.

How REAP Works

Once you have entered all the pertinent details of a property, including the purchase price, rental income, vacancy rate, property taxes, management fees, maintenance costs, home owners association fees, and the mortgage details, REAP will generate seven reports (numeric as well as graphical) to provide an indication of how the property is likely to perform. The reports include details on the cash-on-cash returns (both before and after tax) and the internal rate of return.

System Requirements

- Windows 95/98/ME/2000/NT4.0/XP/Vista
- 133 Mhz or faster Pentium
- 32 MB of RAM

- CD-ROM drive
- Mouse

The REAP software comes in a PC version only. Mac/Apple users will need software such as Parallels or Boot Camp to run REAP on your Mac.

Delivery Information

The REAP software can be delivered physically or electronically. The physical delivery is shipped to you on a CD-ROM (US$495.00). The electronic delivery is sent to you via an e-mail message (US$445.00). The e-mail message contains a link for downloading the program, as well as the serial number needed for registration.

An electronic purchase of REAP will be processed within one standard (U.S.) business day (Monday–Friday, except holidays). A CD-ROM purchase of REAP will be processed within one standard (U.S.) business day (Monday–Friday, except holidays) and shipped via a two-day delivery service. All international orders of REAP will be the electronic version, not the CD-ROM version.

Satisfaction Guarantee

In accordance with industry standards and Property Prosperity policies, no returns will be accepted for software.

Index